THE RIGHT WORD

W.S. Fowler

Nelson

Thomas Nelson and Sons Ltd
Nelson House   Mayfield Road
Walton-on-Thames   Surrey
KT12 5PL   UK

51 York Place
Edinburgh
EH1 3JD   UK

Thomas Nelson (Hong Kong) Ltd
Toppan Building 10/F
22A Westlands Road
Quarry Bay   Hong Kong

Distributed in Australia by

Thomas Nelson Australia
480 La Trobe Street
Melbourne   Victoria 3000
and in Sydney, Brisbane, Adelaide and Perth

ISBN 0–17–555688–1
NCN 73–ELP–9335–01

Designed and typeset by DP Press, Sevenoaks, Kent
Printed in Hong Kong

Contents

Section Two

Key to structural abbreviations

Index to Part B — Verbs

Introduction

Aims

In some ways vocabulary has been a neglected area in English language teaching in recent years. In concentrating their efforts on grammatical accuracy or authentic communication, teachers can easily overlook the fact that the source of many mistakes or of students being unable to express themselves in English is quite simply that they do not know the right words. The aim of this book is to remedy the deficiency for students at intermediate levels leading up to that of Cambridge First Certificate.

It is universally recognised nowadays that new vocabulary is best learnt in context. Even those course books that adopt a thematic approach, however, cannot contextualise in a natural way all the words students are likely to need. If authentic texts are used, it is evident that the writer, not having foreign students in mind, will not include all the necessary vocabulary for students to carry out spoken or written tasks for themselves and at the same time will present students with many items that are not of immediate practical use and have to be looked up in a dictionary. The object of this book is to concentrate on vocabulary items that are practical and in most cases essential to intermediate students. It can be used either as an independent source of new vocabulary or in conjunction with course books in order to fill the inevitable lexical gaps.

Content

The book consists of two parts, the first teaching and providing the means for practising about 1,000 nouns, almost all of which fall within the lexical demands of the Cambridge First Certificate examination, the second dealing with almost 200 common verbs. Each part is divided into two sections. Unless students are enrolled in an intensive course, the coverage of the first section in each part corresponds to the demands of a Pre-First Certificate course, and that of the second section to a level equivalent to a First Certificate course. The vocabulary areas and tasks embodied in practice exercises have been graded accordingly.

Nouns

Nouns make up about three-quarters of the vocabulary items students need to learn at this stage. This is self-evident when we consider that for a relatively simple task such as describing a room, some 20 items may be required; students will already know 'chair' and 'table', but may not readily produce items such as 'fireplace', 'lamp shade', 'rug', 'sideboard' or 'wallpaper', and may confuse 'floor' with 'ground'.

Such words, where they are new vocabulary items or only half-recognised, are best learnt in groups associated with a common theme. It is clearly easier to understand and remember words such as 'wardrobe' and to distinguish between 'sheets' and 'blankets', 'pillows' and 'cushions', from seeing a drawing of a bedroom and subsequently practising the words in the classroom than by coming across any of these items in isolation.

The first 18 units of the book (Part A) are therefore devoted almost entirely to nouns associated by means of a common topic. Students can work through them in order, bearing in mind what I have already said about the book being used for the duration of two courses; alternatively, if the book is used in conjunction with a course book, teachers can use the Contents List to focus on given areas. For detailed notes on use of the material, see below.

Adjectives

On the whole, students at intermediate level are unlikely to benefit from being taught a large number of adjectives beyond the basic ones (beautiful/ugly; tall/short, etc.) they already know. The precision that the use of the correct adjective gives to written work can in my view only be acquired by native speakers through wide reading and for foreign learners such items are more appropriate to a more advanced level. The exceptions are adjectives used to describe people's physical characteristics, and personality, and these have therefore been extensively presented and practised in the first unit.

Verbs

Verbs present a totally different problem for foreign learners. They must not only be distinguished semantically but also confront the learner with structural difficulties in many cases. Whereas, in the case of nouns, the student must simply learn to identify an object with a name in English, verbs are already known but do not always correspond to the apparent equivalents in the student's own language, and appear in different structural combinations. Many languages possess only one common verb for the meanings of 'do' and 'make', for example, and this verb may also be used where in English we use another (e.g. 'take a photograph').

Whereas nouns can be grouped in thematic terms, verbs do not form natural groups except in such cases as the many verbs used for different ways of walking – 'march', 'stride', 'stroll', etc. – which fall, for the most part, outside the scope of this book. I have therefore grouped them according to areas of potential confusion, in part because of first-language interference. In each case, I have provided a grid showing the most frequently encountered structures (but not all) and have given examples of usage. Structures marked (X) are fairly uncommon and have been included for reference purposes rather than as models. Where idiomatic rather than strictly semantic considerations govern the use of one verb rather than another, I have listed the associations. A key to the numbered structural abbreviations is provided at the back of the book. I have also defined the meanings of the verbs, pointed out structural difficulties and highlighted common problems and errors.

The errors may be most commonly found in the work of students whose first language is of Latin origin, although I have endeavoured to draw attention to mistakes made by other foreign learners. The reason is that English speakers over the centuries have most frequently borrowed from Latin and changed or restricted the original meaning; 'elect' in English means 'to choose by voting', but is not used to mean 'choose' in other contexts. As a result, students should pay attention to errors they have a tendency to make themselves but ignore those they do not recognise.

A thematic approach to the presentation of nouns implies that most of the items included are the names of objects. Consequently I have presented nouns that derive from verbs and are often abstract in character ('hope', 'expectation', etc.) in the section on verbs, showing the derivation and semantic relationship.

How to use this book

Part A – Nouns, Section One

As already stated, Part A is made up of 18 topic-based units, which can be dealt with either consecutively over two courses leading up to Cambridge First Certificate or as individual units in conjunction with themes covered in a course book.

The first nine units (in Section One) deal with people, dress, houses, shopping and transport, and considerable use is made here of illustrations in the presentation. In each case, students are first given the opportunity to recognise vocabulary items, most frequently by means of labelling drawings correctly, and are then invited to use them for themselves, and are finally provided with a revision exercise to check that the new items have been learnt. As preparation for conversation tasks and written homework deriving from a course book, the aim is that even if students have not grasped every item taught, they will still have an invaluable source of reference, a visual check-list of the vocabulary they need.

In my experience, the best way of handling labelling exercises such as Unit 1, Exercise 1, is for students to do them in pencil at home before class. Since all the items required are listed alphabetically and they will know several of them, the unfamiliar ones are narrowed down to a choice between the few words remaining. Memory of a previous context may then supply the answers, which should be confirmed in class. Teachers can then practise items as they think best, by asking questions, inviting students to draw figures on the board and modify them, etc. The revision exercises may be done either in class or as homework.

Exercises such as Unit 1, Exercise 4, where students are asked to match contrasting adjectives, clearly lend themselves to subsequent practice of an open-ended kind in which students describe people they know or famous people whose names and characteristics are thought to be familiar to the whole class.

Throughout the book I have used what seemed to me to be the most effective way of teaching the relevant vocabulary items but have made the exploitation flexible.

At all times, however, it is clear that the vocabulary should be related as far as possible to students' own experience. The family tree of the Norton family (Unit 3) is a starting-point for students to construct their own family trees and practise the vocabulary by explaining the relationships; the flat depicted in Unit 4 can give rise to descriptions of students' own flats or houses or ideal houses; the map of the facilities provided by the town of Farley (Unit 5) can be used as a basis for maps of their own towns or districts; the units dealing with transport offer the opportunity for them to explain to the class journeys they have made themselves.

Part A – Nouns, Section Two

The topics here are more specific and less easily presented in visual terms. To a considerable extent I have made use of exercises establishing relationships, such as Unit 9, Exercise 4; exercises forming categories (e.g. Unit 10, Exercise 1, fruit and vegetables); matching exercises; and, above all, dialogues and texts contextualising items and aimed at developing the very important skill in reading comprehension of deriving the meaning of unfamiliar words from a context. The unfamiliar words are printed in different type to attract students' attention.

The majority of these exercises can be done either as homework, prior to exploitation in the classroom, or in class, but I strongly recommend that students should attempt exercises in continuous prose before coming to class. The value of such passages as those on different kinds of school (Unit 18) is lost if students retain the habit of expecting the teacher to provide a translation or definition of every word that is new. The context exists to give the student enough information to make an informed guess; such guesses, when confirmed in the classroom, stick in students' minds much better than translations or definitions copied down in a notebook without mental effort.

Part B – Verbs

The nature of the items and the need to practise correct forms and avoid structural errors necessarily make this part on verbs more academic and less susceptible to classroom exploitation except through the exercises provided. Teachers can either work through the verb groups from beginning to end or concentrate on verbs that have proved a source of error as they come up. The order of presentation within each of the two sections of this part is alphabetical and arbitrary; the grading is limited to separating the verbs into Pre-First Certificate and First Certificate level in the two sections.

To a considerable extent, this part of the book should be regarded as a reference section as much as a source of practice exercises. Teachers should draw students' attention to the index and encourage them, when they have doubts in written work, to consult the relevant group of verbs and information provided before writing one verb rather than another. It may be argued that few young students are prepared to make this effort, but the alternative is more and more remedial work; if students consistently confuse 'rob' and 'steal', for example, it is necessary to do an exercise showing them the difference, but those who continue to make the same mistake afterwards should simply be directed to the explanation and examples given.

Conclusion

No vocabulary book of this kind can hope to teach and practise every item students may need. The criterion I have applied is nevertheless that the items presented are practical and fall within the lexical range of the Cambridge First Certificate examination; as such, they can be defined as useful, indeed essential, vocabulary for intermediate students. It is my hope that as a result the acquisition of the vocabulary needed to carry out spoken and written tasks at this level will be less time-consuming and more rewarding because the learning process will be more effectively controlled.

Will Fowler, Barcelona, August 1986

Part A – Nouns

SECTION ONE

Unit 1
People

1 Look at the drawing, and name each of the numbered physical features, using the list below.

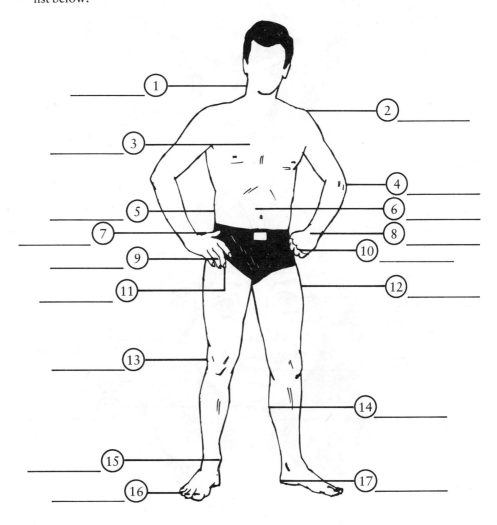

Choose from this list:
ankle calf chest elbow finger fist heel knee nail neck shoulder
stomach thigh thumb toe waist wrist

2 Now look at the two faces drawn here and name the physical features, using the list below.

18 _____

19 _____

20 _____

22 _____

21 _____

23 _____

24 _____

25 _____

26 _____

27 _____

28 _____

29 _____

30 _____

31 _____

32 _____

Choose from this list:
bald head beard cheek chin curly hair eyebrow eyelashes eyelids
forehead freckles jaw lip moustache throat wrinkles

3 Study the table below, showing adjectives and expressions we use to describe people. In some cases, these are used only for men or only for women. Note that we seldom use the less attractive words for people we know and like or we qualify them: 'He's not very tall.' (He's rather short.) or 'She's not very pretty.' (She's rather plain.)

	Men	Women
Age	old elderly middle-aged young . . . looks about (30)	
Height	tall of average (medium) height short	
Figure	broad-shouldered . . . has a good figure muscular well-built	
Shape	fat thin (critical) plump slim (favourable)	
Hair	bald	blonde brunette
	dark-haired fair-haired red-haired long short straight curly wavy	
Face	round long square oval wrinkled freckled	
Complexion	tanned pale sallow fresh	
Nose	long hooked snub (flattened)	
Lips	thin full	

Use adjectives from those listed above to complete this description of a man.

He used to be quite good-looking when he was y_____. He was t_____ and s_____ – he looked so elegant in evening dress! He used to play a lot of games then, so he was t_____ from spending so much time in the open air, and of course he was powerfully-built, m_____ and b_____-s_____. He had a mass of c_____ hair and like most r_____-h_____ people, a pleasant, f_____ face, with a funny little s_____ nose, and f_____ lips, as if he wanted to kiss you. I'm afraid you wouldn't recognise him now! He's only m_____-a_____but he looks about 60! Of course when men lose their hair and go b_____, it always adds years to their real age, but his face is lined and w_____ now, and since he gave up sport, he has put on a lot of weight, so he's rather f_____. Apart from that, sitting in that office all day has given him a p_____, unhealthy complexion. Even his lips look t_____ now; I expect he's got false teeth.

Describe someone in the class, using the vocabulary you have seen above. Put your descriptions in a hat, take it in turns to draw them out and say who you think is being described, giving your reasons.

4 Match the favourable adjectives on the left with the corresponding unfavourable adjectives or phrase on the right. Write the appropriate number in the right-hand column to match the letter on the left.

1	ambitious	a	dim, stupid
2	amusing, entertaining	b	disagreeable
3	beautiful (woman); handsome (man)	c	dull, boring
4	bright, intelligent, clever	d	having no sense of humour
5	calm	e	hypocritical
6	cheerful	f	lacking in initiative
7	even-tempered	g	lazy, idle
8	generous	h	mean
9	good-looking	i	miserable, depressing
10	hard-working	j	moody
11	humorous, witty	k	narrow-minded
12	pleasant, charming	l	plain
13	polite	m	quick-tempered
14	self-confident, outgoing	n	rude
15	sensitive	o	shy, reserved
16	sincere	p	ugly
17	smart	q	unfeeling
18	tolerant	r	untidy

Which of the five characteristics mentioned do you think are the most important in a friend? Which five characteristics do you dislike most in other people? Use the adjectives and phrases given to describe the personality of someone you know.

Revision

Complete the sentences, using the correct word or phrase from those you have seen above. To help you, the first letter of each word is given.

1 Sportsmen usually suffer injuries of some kind sooner or later. Tennis players sprain their w_____, or they get 'tennis e_____'. Footballers break their t_____, or pull muscles in their t_____, or their opponents kick their a_____. Even goalkeepers fracture their f_____ or t_____ saving goals. That's why I play chess!
Yes, but if you spend hours leaning over a table like that, biting your n_____ with anxiety, you'll finish up with a stiff n_____ and round s_____.

2 The cosmetics firms spend their time trying to get people to change their appearance. If girls are dark-haired, they persuade them to dye their hair and become b_____. If their hair is straight, they will make it 'naturally' w_____.
They can make s_____ complexions the colour of peaches and cream. They give you false e_____, and pluck your e_____ if they are too heavy. If you have a h_____ nose, they will straighten it. If you have t_____ lips you can learn to suck in your c_____s to make them look f_____.
It's the same for men nowadays. You can go to clinics where they will stop you from going b_____. You can do exercises to become b_____-shouldered. And with a lamp you can become t_____ without going outdoors.
But the biggest craze these days is that all girls must be s_____. In Grandfather's day, men liked women to be p_____; their idea of a good figure was different. But now, if I looked like that, Jack would say: 'You're getting f_____. Why don't you go on a diet?'

Unit 2
Clothes

1 Look at the drawing of Andrew and his wife, Barbara, below, and decide what they are wearing. Name each of the numbered features, using the list that follows.

Choose from this list:
belt blouse bracelet button collar cuff cuff-link gloves handkerchief high-heeled shoe jacket jumper necklace overcoat raincoat shirt skirt sleeve stocking suit tie trousers waistcoat

Which articles of clothing are likely to be made of the following?
cotton wool nylon leather silk mixtures of other materials with artificial fibres

App nº ①

2 Now look at the drawings of their children, Carol and David. Name each of the numbered features, using the list that follows.

Choose from this list:
basketball boot gym shoe jeans pullover shorts sock T-shirt tights
track suit top

Use the list of items you have numbered above to describe how you are dressed yourself or the clothes of another person in the room.

3 Look at the drawing of other items of clothing, and name each of the numbered features, using the list that follows. Then answer the questions.

Choose from this list:
bikini bra briefs cardigan dress knickers pyjamas scarf slippers swimming trunks swimsuit vest

What are the differences between the following?
a boots, slippers and shoes   *b* suits and jackets   *c* jumpers, pullovers and cardigans   *d* socks and stockings   *e* blouses and shirts   *f* dresses and suits *g* bikinis and swimsuits   *h* bracelets and necklaces.

Which of the following would you wear mainly above the waist, mainly below the waist, both above and below?
There are five items of clothing in each group. Make three groups of five.
bikini briefs dress pyjamas pullover scarf shirt shorts skirt suit swimsuit tights trunks vest waistcoat

15

When we speak of two objects that always go together, we call them a pair (e.g. **a pair of shoes**). We also speak of **a pair of trousers**, thinking of the two legs. Find the other thirteen pairs, not counting **shoes** and **trousers**, among the items of clothing and other objects you have seen in the drawings above.

The most common patterns of clothes are **striped, spotted** and **checked**. Find any clothes in the drawings with these patterns.

4 Read the following dialogue, making sure that you understand the meaning of the words and phrases in different type. Then practise, as indicated below.

Marion	Hello, I'm looking for a **sweater**.
Joan	Certainly, madam. What kind of sweater do you want?
Marion	A **woollen** one.
Joan	What **size** are you, madam? Medium?
Marion	Yes. And I want a plain colour, not one with a **pattern**. That green one looks quite nice. Can I **try it on**?
Joan	Certainly, madam. (*a moment later*) Oh, that **fits** you perfectly. It's certainly your size.
Marion	Yes, but now that I've **got it on**, I don't think it **suits** me. Have you got the same thing in a different **shade** of green?

Practise buying an article of clothing from a shop. Take into account the following: material (woollen, cotton, leather, etc.), colour and shade (light blue, dark green, etc.), pattern (spotted, checked, striped, etc.), size (does it fit you?), taste (does it suit you?).

Revision

Complete the sentences, using the words or phrases you have seen above. To help you, the first letter of each word is given.

1 It's very cold today. You'd better put your o_____ on and wrap a s_____ round your neck.
2 Can I help you, sir?
  Yes, I'd like a pair of t_____s, if you've got them in a strong material. Otherwise, it will have to be a pair of j_____s.
3 That's a lovely b_____, Jane.
  Yes, I bought it to go with my new cardigan. It's plain and simple but it will set off the c_____ pattern, and anyway, I can always wear it at home with a j_____ over it.
4 Good heavens, I'm tired. It was a hard day at the office today. I'm going to get this s_____ and c_____ and t_____ off and change into something more comfortable. My feet are killing me. Have you seen my s_____ anywhere?
5 I always feel evening dress is like a uniform – dinner j_____, bow t_____, dress s_____, with two inches of c_____ showing so that people can admire your c_____-l_____, white h_____ in the breast pocket, patent l_____ shoes, and all that sort of thing!
  But for girls it's not. It's a great chance to buy a lovely long d_____ and wear it only two or three times!

Unit 3
Family relationships

1 Study the family tree of the Norton family, and then answer the questions that
follow. The ages of those living are given in brackets below each name.

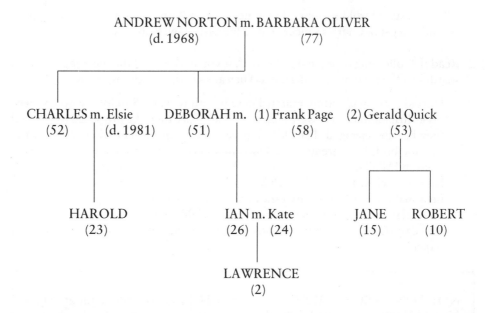

In Britain it is normal for the wife to take the husband's name, and for the children
to have only the father's surname. So Barbara is Mrs Barbara Norton, and
Deborah, when she was single, was called Deborah Norton.

What are the full names of the following: Deborah, Harold, Ian, Jane, Lawrence?

Which member of the family is a widow? Which is a widower?

What relation are the following members of the family to Barbara? Match the
name to the relationship.

Charles	daughter
Deborah	granddaughter
Gerald	grandson
Harold	great-grandson
Jane	son
Lawrence	son-in-law

What relation are the following members of the family to Deborah? Match the
name to the relationship.

Barbara	brother
Charles	ex-husband
Frank	husband
Gerald	nephew
Harold	daughter
Jane	mother

What relation are the following members of the family to Ian? Match the name to the relationship.

Barbara   cousin
Charles   father
Frank   grandmother
Gerald   sister
Harold   stepfather
Jane   uncle

Who is/was Harold's aunt, Lawrence's grandfather, Frank's stepdaughter, Gerald's stepson, Charles's niece, Kate's father-in-law, Robert's sister-in-law?

2 Read the following texts, making sure that you understand the meaning of all the words in different type or underlined. Then answer the questions below.

Harold Norton is **getting married** next month **to** Mary Sutcliffe, who has been his **girlfriend** since they were **teenagers**. Last Christmas, he **proposed to** her, and they became **engaged**. Harold's **fiancée** became an **orphan** when she was five because both her **parents** were killed in an accident but she has two brothers, Tom and William. The **elder** brother, Tom, went to school with Harold, so they have been **close friends** since **childhood**. At the moment, Harold and Mary are busy making out a list of **invitations** to the **wedding**. They are going to invite all their **relatives** and a number of friends and **neighbours**.

The day after the wedding, the following announcement appeared in the local paper:

NORTON SUTCLIFFE — Harold Norton, son of Mr Charles Norton of 26 Pine Close, Farley, and the late Mrs Elsie Norton to Mary Elizabeth Sutcliffe, daughter of the late Mr Ernest and Mrs Jean Sutcliffe, of 119 Oak Avenue, Farley, at St. Andrew's Church. The marriage service was conducted by the Reverend John Wales, Vicar of Farley. The bride was given away by her brother, Mr Tom Sutcliffe, and the bridesmaids were her cousin, Miss Sybil Chase, and the bridegroom's cousin, Miss Jane Quick. At the reception in the King's Arms, Mr Gerald Quick proposed the health of the bride and groom, and the bridegroom replied on behalf of the happy couple. The best man, the bridegroom's cousin, Mr Ian Page, was in charge of the arrangements, and afterwards made an amusing speech and read out telegrams from friends abroad.

Put the following in chronological order and then find the female equivalents: fiancé, husband, boyfriend, bridegroom.

Compare the names given to a couple at different stages in their relationship with those given to them in your country. Are there any differences?

Is the description of the marriage and the wedding reception here similar to what would happen in your country? What are the responsibilities of the bride's father, the bridesmaids, the best man?

Revision

Complete the sentences, using the correct word or phrase from those you have seen above. To help you, the first letter of each word is given. You may refer to the family tree of the Norton family, and the account of the marriage and wedding reception.

A wedding I have attended, by Jane Quick (4b)
My c_____, Harold, got married last weekend and I was
a b_____ at the w_____. All the family were very
happy, because we have known the b_____, Mary
Sutcliffe, for a long time, and Harold had been going out
with her for a year before they became e_____.
    Mary's p_____s died in a car crash when she
was very young, so she became an o_____, but her
b_____ Tom is a kind man and has always looked after
her. When Harold and Mary were making out the list of
i_____s for the wedding, of course they invited all
the r_____s and some friends and n_____s, but
we wondered if my m_____'s first h_____, my
s_____ Mr Page, would accept, because he lives in
Newcastle and my g_____ has never forgiven him
because of the d_____. But he did come, perhaps
because my stepbrother Ian – thats his s_____ – was
going to be the b_____ m_____. I wondered
what my f_____ would say, but Daddy is very
sensible and he said he hadn't got any time for silly
family quarrels. Everyone was very happy during the
m_____ service, except my U_____ Charles, the
b_____'s father. He was a little sad – I suppose because
my A_____ Elsie died a few years ago and he was
thinking about her.
    Afterwards, we went to the r_____ at the King's
Arms and had a big lunch and everyone made speeches.
Then the b_____ cut the cake, with Harold helping
her, and they went off to their honeymoon in Ibiza
and left us to dance all evening. My Uncle
Charles cheered up and came up to me and said,
'I must come and dance with my n_____, the prettiest
girl in the room', so I felt very pleased.

Unit 4
Houses, flats and furniture

1 Read the following text, making sure that you understand the meaning of all the words in different type.

> Tom and Betty used to live in a big old house. **Downstairs**, on the **ground floor**, they had a **living room**, which they also used as the **dining room**, a room Tom used as a **study**, and a big **kitchen**, with a table and chairs, that they could use as a **breakfast room**; it had a **laundry room** leading off it, where they had the washing machine. There was also a flight of stone **steps** leading down from the hall to the **cellar** in the **basement**. **Upstairs**, at the top of the **staircase**, leading off the **landing**, were the **bathroom** and the **toilet** and three **bedrooms**. At the end of the landing was a door, and behind it, a ladder that went up inside the roof to the **attic**. They had turned that into a **playroom** for the children.

Where did the different members of the family do the following?
a have breakfast b have dinner c write business letters d play games e do the washing-up f wash the clothes g have a wash h store wine

Now Tom and Betty have moved into a top-floor flat. There are windows on two sides, and on the inside, there is a central courtyard open to the sky, so the cooking smells do not upset the neighbours. Look at the plan, and decide how they distributed the eleven rooms in the flat, including a study, a playroom for the children, and a laundry room. Then imagine you are Tom or Betty showing guests around the flat, as they come into the hall. Take them round the flat, making any appropriate comments, such as: 'The kitchen's large, so we usually have breakfast here . . .'

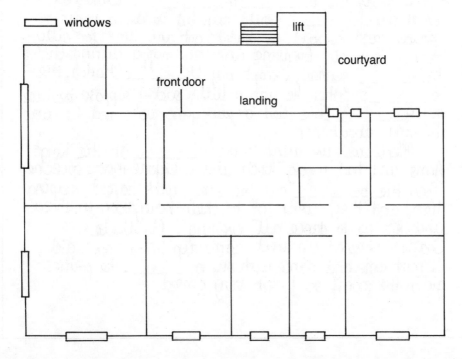

2 Look at the drawings of the living room, the bedroom and the kitchen, and see how many of the numbered objects you can name correctly. Use the list of words given as a guide.

Choose from this list:
armchair bookshelves ceiling curtains cushion electric fire fireplace
floor french windows lamp shade mantelpiece ornament radiator rug
sideboard sofa standard lamp tablecloth table mat vase wallpaper

21

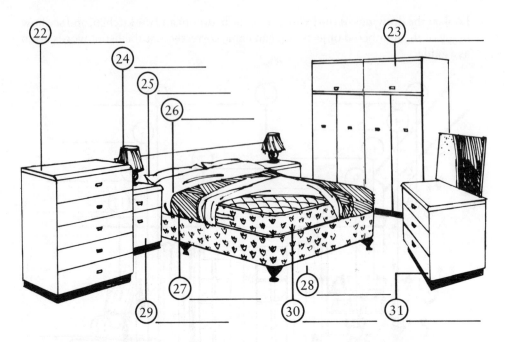

Choose from this list:
bedside lamp bedside table blanket carpet chest of drawers dressing table
mattress pillow sheet wardrobe

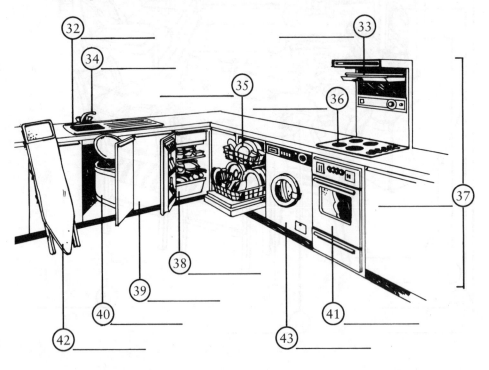

Choose from this list:
cooker cupboard dishwasher fridge grill hotplate ironing board oven
sink tap washing machine waste bin

Describe any of the rooms you have been looking at. Is it like your living-room or bedroom or kitchen at home? Describe one of the rooms at home, using the words you have learnt.

3 How many of the numbered objects of household equipment can you name? Use the list of words given as a guide.

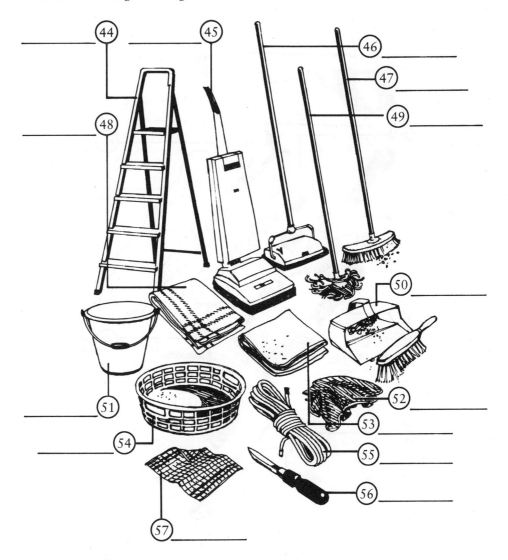

Choose from this list:
broom bucket carpet sweeper cloth clothes basket clothes line dishcloth
duster dustpan and brush mop peeler stepladder teatowel vacuum cleaner

Which objects would you need to do the following household jobs?
a clean the windows *b* do the washing *c* do the washing up *d* dust the
furniture *e* sweep the floor *f* wash the floors
Describe in detail the actions of:
doing the washing up by hand; washing the floor.

4 How many of the tools and other equipment pictured below can you name? Use the list of words given as a guide.

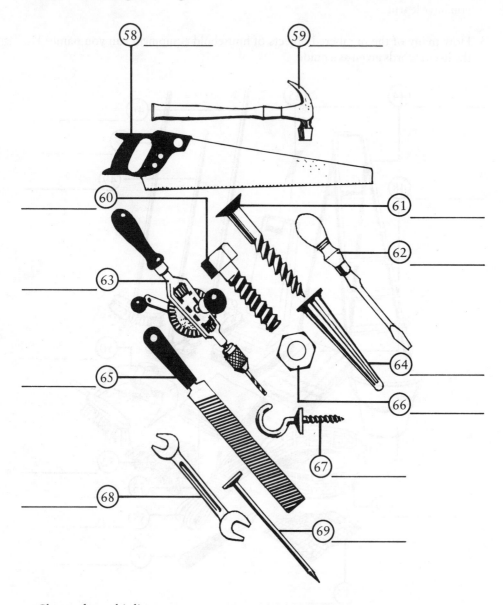

Choose from this list:
bolt drill file hammer hook nail nut plug saw screw screwdriver
spanner

Which objects would you use to do the following things?
a cut wood   *b* remove rough edges   *c* knock nails in   *d* screw something to the
wall or unscrew it   *e* make a hole in the wall   *f* separate a nut and a bolt
Describe the actions in hanging up a picture, mentioning the tools you would use
to fix it to the wall.
What would you need to do to make bookshelves from some wood you had
bought, and then fix them to the wall?

Revision

Complete the sentences, using the correct word or phrase from those you have seen above. To help you, the first letter of each word is given.

1 I've left a note for the children on the m_____ over the fireplace.
2 You should wipe your shoes on the doormat as you come in, instead of walking all over my nice, clean c_____.
3 There must be a leak in the r_____ somewhere. Water is dripping through the c_____ in the bedroom.
4 You must have been very warm in bed last night. Your p_____ is wet. Why didn't you take the b_____ off?
5 Hang your coat up in the w_____, and then you can help me by laying the table. The t_____ and the table m_____ are in the s_____, with the knives and forks.
6 Would you mind helping me with the washing-up? Throw the rubbish in the w_____ b_____ and put the dirty plates in the s_____. There's some washing-up liquid in the c_____. Here's a d_____ and a t_____.
7 This kitchen is in a terrible state. I'll sweep up the dust first with a b_____ and d_____ and b_____, and then I'll have to go over the f_____ with a m_____ and a b_____ of water, and wash it thoroughly.
8 I'm not used to this new h_____ I've bought. I can't knock the n_____s in straight.

Unit 5
Finding a place to live

1 Look at the drawings of different kinds of accommodation and say which is which:
a block of flats   a bungalow   a cottage   a detached house   a semi-detached house
terraced houses

What materials do you think the builder used to build them: brick, concrete or
stone?
Where would you choose to live if you were:
a a young couple with three children?   b a couple without children?   c a retired
couple?   d a young person living alone?   e an old person living alone?
Give reasons for your choice.

2 Look at this house and garden and name each of the numbered features, using the list below.

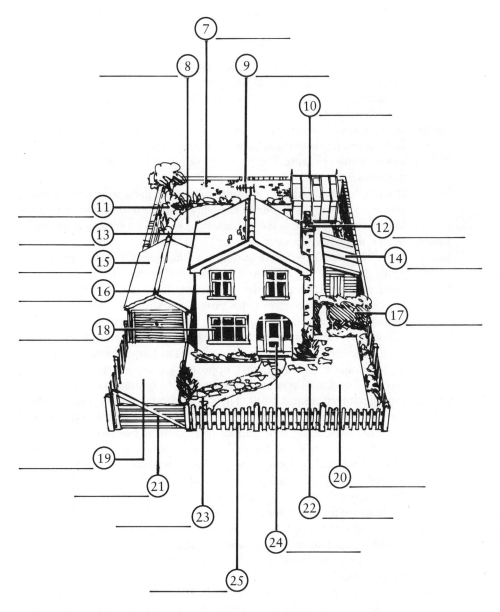

Choose from this list:
aerial back garden bedroom window chimney driveway fence
flower beds front door front garden garage gate greenhouse
ground floor windows hedge lawn path roof shed wall

What materials were used for the following?
a the fence *b* the garage *c* the gate *d* the greenhouse *e* the roof *f* the wall
g the windows
brick glass stone tiles wood
What is the difference between a fence, a hedge and a wall?

3 James Nash and his wife Susan are coming to work in Farley, and are looking for a house. This is part of a conversation with Mr Reeve, an estate agent in Market Square, Farley. Read the conversation and look at the map of Farley. The places mentioned are all on the map.

James   . . . I'm going to be the branch manager at the National Bank on the right over there, and Susan's going to teach at the new **primary school** between London Road and South Street. Then we have to think of the children. Peter will be going to Farley School, and we'd like Anne to go to a **playschool**, if there's one nearby.

Susan   So we want a house big enough for the four of us, on the edge of town, but not too far from the schools, and preferably near a bus route to the **town centre**, because I suppose parking is difficult here, with the narrow streets.

Reeve   It's not too bad. There's a **multi-storey car park** near the **shopping centre** on the opposite side of the square, and another one behind the **big office block** you can see on the left. How well do you know Farley?

James   We've only been here once or twice.

Reeve   I see. Well, come over here and look at the map. Of course property is more expensive on the south side of the town, which is really the residential area. Over in the north-east, there are a lot of **factories** further up the road from the **power station**, and up towards the **industrial estate**. But, coming down South Street you can see Farley School, with its **playing fields**, and beyond that Farley Park. That's quite near your **primary school**, madam. The larger houses really begin at St. Andrew's Church, just opposite, on the corner of Stockton Avenue. Stockton Avenue is mostly big old houses, well-built by the same architect around 1900. They're in good condition but of course the upkeep is expensive, and they may be too large for you. Most of them are divided up now and let to tenants as **bed-sitters**. However, further south, on Wood Lane, there's a **new housing estate** on a large plot of land, and opposite there's a **playschool** with a large **playground**, as well as Stockton Park nearby. That would still be within walking distance of the primary school.

James   What about the bus service into town?

Reeve   That's all right. The buses from the outlying villages, Wood End and Hoddington, stop in Wood Lane, and they come right in to the **central bus station** at the back of this building, so it's only three minutes' walk to the bank.

Susan   I don't fancy a housing estate much. It would be like the suburbs of London, where we live now. I thought we might find something on the outskirts, nearer the country.

Reeve   Well, they're building some lovely houses in Chestnut Lane, right on the **town boundary**, but of course that's a good deal further out . . .

Use the map to find the following and give each its correct number:
the primary school   the playschool   the industrial estate   factories
the power station   the new housing estate   the shopping centre
the big office block   two multi-storey car parks   the central bus station
the town boundary   the school playing fields.

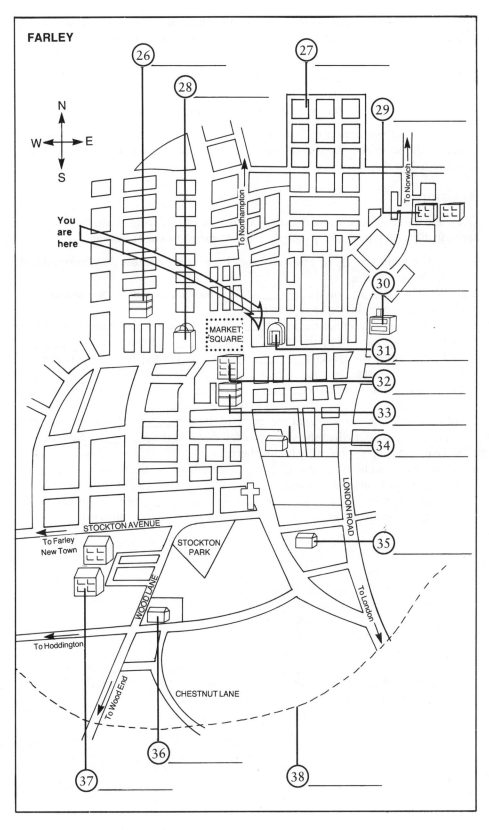

FARLEY

You are here

To Northampton

To Norwich

MARKET SQUARE

STOCKTON AVENUE

To Farley New Town

STOCKTON PARK

WOOD LANE

LONDON ROAD

To London

To Hoddington

To Wood End

CHESTNUT LANE

On which side of the square in the map is the estate agent's office, and which side is the National Bank? Which streets are on the bus route from Wood End to the central bus station?

Why do you think the upkeep of the houses in Stockton Avenue is expensive, and why have they been let to tenants as bed-sitters? Are James and Susan going to be tenants? How many rooms would you expect to find in a bed-sitter?

Where would you expect to find the suburbs of a city? Why does Anne prefer to live on the outskirts? What are the names of the outlying villages, and why is this term used for them?

Revision

Complete the sentences, using the correct word or phrase from those you have seen above in different type. To help you, the first letter in each word is given.

1 They've bought a b_____ now that they have retired because they find it difficult to climb stairs.
2 Two of the t_____ on the r_____ were blown down in the storm last night, so I'm going up the ladder to replace them.
3 I found a stray dog sheltering in the g_____ this morning. I must have left the door open. He ran out across the flower b_____ and through the h_____, and jumped over the garden w_____ before I could catch him. At least he didn't break any panes of glass.
4 He works in that big twelve-s_____ office b_____ in the centre of the town, on the eleventh f_____. It's just as well there's a lift.
5 Alison is three now so she's started going to the p_____. That's until she goes to p_____school when she's five. She fell down in the p_____ the other day and cut her knee, but she's very happy there.
6 He lives in an old house on the o_____ of the town, on the town b_____. It's pleasant to look out and see the fields but the u_____ of an old building like that must be expensive. He wanted to divide it into b_____ but it's not easy to get t_____ who are willing to live so far from the bus r_____ into town.

Unit 6
Shopping

1 In Britain people go to buy the things or obtain the services listed in the left-hand column at one of the places listed on the right. Match the articles or services on the left with the correct places on the right. In some cases, you would go to the same place. Write the appropriate number in the right-hand column to match the letter on the left.

1	to buy aspirin		a	the baker's
2	a book		b	the off-licence
3	cakes		c	the chemist's
4	fish		d	a bookshop
5	flowers		e	the dry-cleaner's
6	fruit		f	the fishmonger's
7	beer		g	the florist's
8	a newspaper		h	the greengrocer's
9	perfume		i	the grocer's
10	a pipe		j	the ironmonger's
11	soup		k	the launderette
12	stamps		l	the laundry
13	sweets		m	the library
14	tools		n	the newsagent's
15	vegetables		o	the tailor's
16	to borrow a book		p	the tobacconist's
17	to have a suit made		q	the Post Office
18	to have your clothes washed			
19	to have a suit cleaned			
20	to wash your own clothes			

Do you buy all these things or obtain these services at the same places in your country?

2 Read the following text, making sure that you understand the meaning of all the words in different type.

My wife loves **window-shopping**. She loves walking up and down in front of shop windows, looking at the **range** of **goods on display**, especially in the new **shopping centre**, where there are a lot of **boutiques** selling their own **designs**. I prefer big **department stores** because all the best-known **products** are **on sale**, and usually **in stock**. If they are **out of stock**, the **shop assistant** can order them for you. Most of the **chain stores** have **branches** in our **shopping centre**. My wife only enjoys going there when they have the **sales** every year and she thinks she can find **bargains**.

Do you like window-shopping? Do you prefer department stores or corner shops, where the shopkeeper knows you and talks to you?

3 Read the text, as for Exercise 2.

> This week Fine Food **Supermarkets** has a whole range of **special offers** for its **customers**. Look at these wonderful bargains! 15p **off** all Tiger **brand** biscuits – look for the familiar tiger **trade mark**! Special **reductions** this week on all Ice-Pack frozen foods! For every three boxes of Splash detergent, a free **sample** of the new after-shave, He-Man! For all **purchases** over £50, a £5 sales **voucher** equivalent to a 10% **discount**.

Can you name the three most popular brands of soft drink in your country? Do they have a trade mark? What does it look like? Are these sales techniques typical of supermarkets where you live? Do shops still offer discounts? If so, for which goods?

4 Read the following notice, as before.

REGULATIONS FOR SHOPPERS

Please leave **shopping** bags at the entrance, and use the **trolleys** and **baskets** provided for your purchases. The assistants at the **check-out counter** will **wrap them up**. Ask for **carrier bags** if you require them.

All purchases must be paid for **in cash**. We regret that we do not accept payment **by cheque** or **by credit card**.

Imagine you are a shop assistant in a supermarket. Develop a short dialogue with a customer who *a* wanted to come in with a shopping bag *b* wants to pay by cheque.

5 *a* Imagine you are buying a hair-dryer. Why would you want to make sure that the package contains: **instructions; a guarantee**? Why would you ask for a **receipt**? If you were buying it as a present, why would you ask for it to be **gift-wrapped**?

 b Imagine you are buying a video. You cannot afford to **pay cash** but the **salesperson** tells you that you can buy it on **hire purchase**. He tells you what the **monthly instalments** will be. What does he mean?

 c Imagine you are buying some shoes. What size do you want? Why do you need **to try them on**? (To see if they **fit**.) Why are you interested in the **style**? (To see if they **suit** you.)

 d Imagine you are buying a car. The salesperson will not ask you what brand of car you are interested in, but what **make**, and which **model**. He will not ask you for all the money in cash. He may offer you **facilities, on easy terms**. What does he mean?

Develop short dialogues for each of these situations, using the phrases in different type you have learned. As the customer, ask questions like: 'Can/May I . . . , please?' 'How much . . . ?'
As the salesperson/shop assistant, ask questions like: 'Would you like . . . ?'

Revision

Complete the sentences, using the correct word or phrase from those you have seen above in different type. To help you, the first letter in each word is given.

1 I'm just going round to the l_____ to do my washing.
2 This isn't the book my mother wanted. I wonder if the b_____ will take it back.
   That depends. Have you got a r_____ to show that you paid for it?
3 My car is a Ford. What m_____ is yours?
4 I'm sorry. This item is out of s_____ at the moment, but we can order it for you.
   I don't understand why it is not on s_____. I've seen it on d_____in your shop window.
5 This is a free s_____ of a new b_____ of toothpaste.
6 Come to our January s_____s! We're offering shoppers all kinds of wonderful b_____s at incredibly low prices. Our store has b_____s all over the country.
7 Please pay the assistant at the c_____-o_____ counter either i_____ cash or b_____ credit card.
8 I'm afraid these shoes don't f_____ me. Can I try o_____ a larger s_____?
9 Before you leave the shop, make sure that the g_____ is signed and dated, and when you reach home with your p_____, read the i_____ before using it.
10 If you are going to pay for the TV by h_____ purchase, I'll let you know what the monthly i_____s will come to.

Unit 7
Road transport

1 Look at the drawing of a car and name each of the numbered features, using the list below.

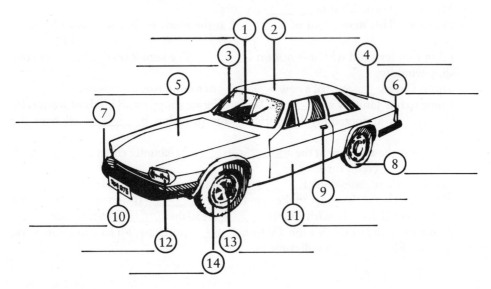

Choose from this list:
bonnet boot bumper door door handle headlight hubcap numberplate
rear light roof tyre wheel windscreen windscreen wiper

2 Look at the drawing of the driving seat and the controls of a car, and name each of the numbered features, using the list on the next page.

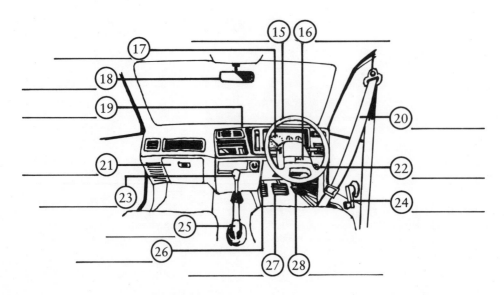

Choose from this list:
accelerator brake clutch dashboard gear lever glove compartment
handbrake horn ignition mirror seat belt speedometer steering wheel
window winder

3 Study this list of vehicles and then answer the questions that follow:
ambulance breakdown truck bus caravan cart coach container lorry
estate car fire engine motor-cycle pick-up scooter tanker tram van
a Which two have no engine?
b Which two have two wheels?
c Which one runs on rails?
d Which three are designed to transport a number of passengers?
e Which one can be used as a house?
f Which two provide essential public services, apart from transport?
g Which one would you need if your car had to be towed to a garage?
h Which one carries petrol?
i Which one is useful for taking a lot of personal belongings with you?
j Which four are built to transport goods?
k Which two of these four have no roof, except over the driver's cabin?
l Which of the other two is larger?
How many of these vehicles have you travelled in or on? What was the purpose of
the journey in each case?

Revision

Complete the sentences, using the correct word or phrase from those you have seen
above. To help you, the first letter of each word is given.

1 Fasten your s_____ b_____, turn on the i_____, press the a_____
gently, look in the m_____ before starting off to make sure no one is coming,
then release the h_____, get into first g_____, release the c_____ and
drive away.
2 We've got a puncture in the front left-hand t_____. I must stop and change the
w_____. There's a spare one in the b_____.
3 When I drove into the back of him, I broke his r_____ l_____. That was the
only damage, apart from denting the b_____ and the n_____, but
fortunately everything under the b_____ was all right, so I could drive away
afterwards.
4 My w_____ w_____s are not working properly. There's a cloth in the
g_____ c_____ in the d_____ there. Could you pass it to me?
5 A_____s and f_____ e_____s were called to the scene of an accident on
the M1 this morning when an articulated c_____ l_____ collided with a
t_____ carrying inflammable gas. The accident occured when the l_____
tried to overtake a c_____ carrying football supporters to Birmingham, and
skidded across the motorway into the path of oncoming traffic. A family whose
c_____ was detached from their car narrowly escaped death.
6 We'll load the furniture into the removal v_____, and some of the small stuff
can go on the back of the p_____. I'll take everything else in the e_____ car,
and you can follow behind on your s_____.
What about Jack?
Oh, we'll fit him in somewhere. Otherwise, he'll have to go by b_____.

35

Unit 8
On the road

1 Look at the drawing and name each of the numbered features, using the list below.

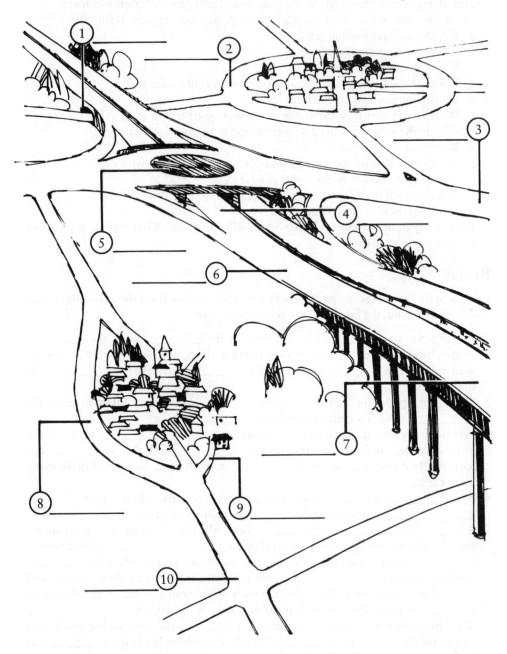

Choose from this list:
bridge bypass crossroads flyover main road motorway roundabout
ring road side road underpass

2 Look at the drawing of the road signs and say what each of them indicates, using the list below.

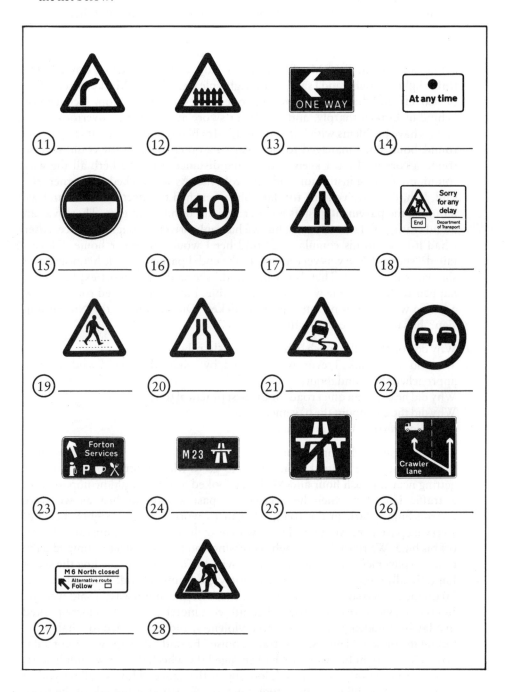

11 _____ 12 _____ 13 _____ 14 _____

15 _____ 16 _____ 17 _____ 18 _____

19 _____ 20 _____ 21 _____ 22 _____

23 _____ 24 _____ 25 _____ 26 _____

27 _____ 28 _____

Choose from this list:
crawler lane   dangerous bend to right   diversion   dual carriageway ends
end of motorway   end of roadworks   level crossing with gates   motorway begins
no entry   no overtaking   no parking   one way street   roadworks   service area
road narrows   speed limit 40 mph   slippery surface   zebra crossing

3 Trevor Andrews is an examiner for people who take driving tests. He is describing his experiences with two learners in the two texts that follow. Read them, making sure you understand the meaning of the words in different type, and then answer the questions.

> The trouble is, you see, that you're not supposed to talk to the drivers except to avoid an **accident**. Take Mrs Bland, a nice lady, *but* . . . We drove down to the **traffic lights** all right, and I said, 'Turn right, please, towards Market Street'. She turned left, and then realised she had gone in the wrong direction. A **coach** just behind us **braked** sharply, and the driver swore at us when he **overtook** us. 'I always have problems with left and right,' Mrs Bland said, as we came up to the **roundabout**. But I managed to **steer** her to a quiet road, so she could **reverse** round a corner. 'I must keep at the same **distance** from the **kerb** all the way round, my **driving instructor** said,' she told me. As we reached the corner, she said, 'Oh, dear, we've gone too far.' She wrenched the **steering wheel** and we mounted the **pavement**, just as a man came out of his front gate. There was an awful **crash**, and I shut my eyes, but we had only driven through his fence. After I had listened to his complaints, I told her I would drive her home. 'Have I failed?' she said. She was very angry. In the end, I **parked** outside her house and she was still arguing. 'There's my husband,' she said. 'You must explain what happened.' So I did. He was quite reasonable, but when I turned round, I saw a **traffic warden** writing out a **parking ticket**. 'Didn't you see the **No Parking sign**?' he said. 'And you a driving examiner!'

a Why do you think the coach behind braked sharply?
b Why do you think Trevor was worried by what Mrs Bland said as they approached the roundabout?
c Why did he choose a quiet road for the first practical test?
d Why did the car mount the pavement?
e How did Trevor get a parking ticket?

> Mr Hogg was much worse, though. He had his own Jaguar, with **L plates** on it. We took the same route. I didn't want to go to Market Street because it was getting near the **rush hour** and Mr Hogg looked as if he would be impatient in a **traffic jam**. But when he **accelerated** past a **minibus** just as we were approaching a **fork** in the road, I began to worry. 'Left or right?' he said, **swerving** past a **cyclist**. 'Left', I said, watching the cyclist in the **mirror** as he fell off his bike. We **roared** over a **zebra crossing** and two **pedestrians** jumped back onto the pavement just in time. '**Slow down**,' I said, 'you're **exceeding the speed limit**. 'Really?' he said, as we passed a lorry going into a **bend**. 'I thought it was 70 on the **main road** out of town'. 'No, that's on the **motorway**,' I said weakly. In no time, we were out of town. I could see a **motel** ahead and a lorry parked in a **lay-by**. Suddenly, the car swerved violently, and we **skidded** to a **halt** as he **put on the brakes**. 'There was a strange noise,' he said. 'Perhaps we've got a **flat tyre**.' He was right but when we had changed the wheel, the car wouldn't start. 'You've **run out of** petrol', I said, looking at the **gauge**. 'How silly!' he said. 'I asked my wife to **fill up** before I **took my test**.' We stood at the side of the road, trying to **flag down** passing motorists. They didn't stop. They thought we were **hitch-hikers**, hoping to get a **lift**. In the end, I came back by bus and said I would tell the nearest **garage**. It was better than coming back with him, though.

f Why did Mr Hogg's car have L plates on it?

g Why did Trevor prefer not to go towards Market Street?
h Why was Mr Hogg wrong to accelerate past the minibus?
i Why did the pedestrians jump back onto the pavement?
j What is the speed limit on the motorway?
k What do you think a motel is? And what is a lay-by?
l Why did the car skid to a halt?
m What do you do if you have a flat tyre?
n Why wouldn't the car start after they had changed the wheel?
o Why did they try to flag down motorists, and why didn't the motorists stop?

Revision

Complete the sentences, using the correct word or phrase from those you have seen above. To help you, the first letter of each word is given. **Note** that five of the statements are false. Decide which statements are false and correct them.

1 A b_____ enables motorists to pass by towns on the m_____ r_____ instead of going through them. A r_____ r_____ goes round the town, allowing you to enter it at the most convenient point.

2 A f_____ goes under the main road while an u_____ goes over it.

3 Never o_____ another car when approaching a b_____ in the road because you cannot see oncoming traffic and may have a head-on c_____.

4 The c_____ l_____ on roads is for lorries and similar traffic.

5 A o_____-w_____ street is one where all traffic must go in the same d_____.

6 The place where the road crosses railway lines is called a junction, or c_____.

7 The s_____ l_____ on motorways in Britain is 70 miles per hour.

8 When you see the t_____ l_____ changing from green to amber, a_____ so you will get through them before they turn red.

9 The r_____ h_____ is the time when most people are going to work or going home. That is why there are so many t_____ j_____s.

10 T_____ w_____s give people tickets if they p_____ where it is not allowed.

11 H_____-h_____ are people who f_____ d_____ motorists to ask them the way.

12 If you get a puncture (or f_____ t_____) you have to change the w_____.

13 When lorry drivers get tired, they usually stop for a time in a l_____-b_____. Some people prefer to spend the night in a m_____.

14 Before starting a long journey, look at the petrol g_____; otherwise, you may r_____ o_____ of petrol.

15 It is dangerous to b_____ sharply on a slippery surface; you may s_____ to one side, causing an a_____, or s_____ and crash into a wall or another car.

16 You only have to s_____ d_____ when approaching a z_____ c_____ if you see a zebra. P_____s seeing a car approaching must stay on the p_____.

Unit 9
Travelling by rail, sea and air

1 Look at the drawing of a train and name each of the numbered features, using the list below.

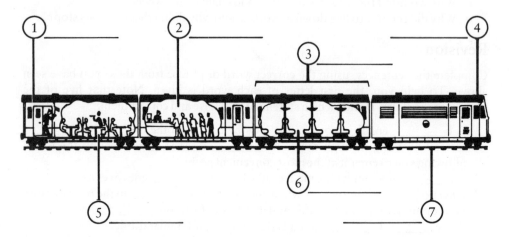

Choose from this list:
buffet carriage compartment dining car engine guard's van rails

If you are travelling on a train, do you prefer a window seat? Does it matter to you if you sit facing the engine or with your back to it? Which do you prefer?

2 Look at the drawing of a liner and name each of the numbered features, using the list below.

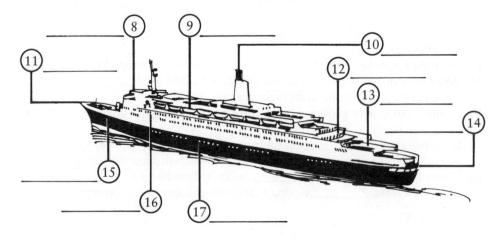

Choose from this list:
bow bridge cabin deck funnel hold lifeboats porthole saloon stern

Have you ever travelled in a ship like this? How long was the voyage? How did you pass the time?

3 Look at the drawing of an airliner and name each of the numbered features, using the list below.

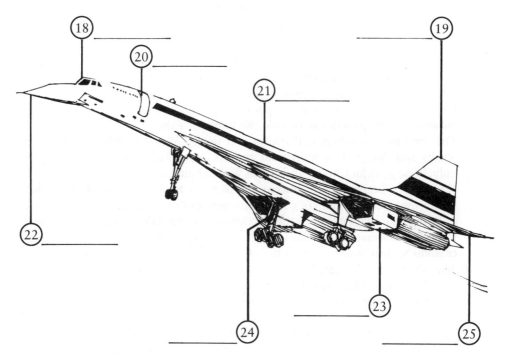

Choose from this list:
cockpit fuselage hatch jet engine nose tail undercarriage wing

What do you like and dislike about flying?

4 The table given below is incomplete in some places. Find the correct words from the list underneath to fill the gaps.

By rail	By sea	By air
_____	ship	aircraft
passenger train	liner	_____
_____	port	airport
platform	quay	_____
journey		flight
catch, get on	embark	_____
_____	disembark	disembark
arrive	dock	_____
depart, leave	_____	take off
engine		_____
engine driver	_____	pilot
_____	gangway	aisle
_____	cargo	_____

Choose from this list:
airliner board bridge captain cockpit corridor departure lounge freight get off goods land sail station train voyage

41

5 Read the following announcements and conversations and decide where you think they are taking place. Note the words and phrases in different type and make sure you understand their meaning. Then answer the questions that follow.

a Welcome to Flight BA 126 from London to Zurich. In accordance with international flying regulations, we ask you to pay attention to the demonstration of the use of **life jackets**. You will find your life jacket under your seat. The **emergency exits** on the aircraft are clearly marked by **arrows** on either side at the front and in the centre of the aircraft. Lunch will be served during the flight, and you will also have the opportunity to purchase **duty-free goods** when the **stewardesses** pass down the **aisle**. We hope you enjoy your flight.

b The train now standing at Platform 7 is the 10.34 for Holyhead, **calling** at Rugby and Crewe. This train is an **express**, composed of first-class **carriages** only. Passengers for Chester and North Wales **change** at Crewe.

c We are now beginning our **descent** and in a few minutes will **land** at London Heathrow. Please fasten your **seat belts**, and put out your cigarettes. Do not unfasten your seat belts until the aircraft comes to a **halt**. Passengers **in transit** for other **destinations** in the United Kingdom are requested to go through **customs** at Heathrow to identify their **luggage**.

d The advantage of this **package tour** is that you have a **courier** with you all the way. Instead of going on a **charter flight**, which is always liable to delay, you go on a normal flight to Belgrade with British Airways. Once you are in Yugoslavia, you can depart from the standard **itinerary** if you want to . . .
Yes, most **tour operators** like to keep people together, like a lot of sheep, but we know that most customers want a certain amount of freedom. Of course, you must realise that you will have to make your own hotel **reservations** if you depart from the standard procedure, and . . .

e This is the **last call** for Flight BA 827 for Rome and Athens. Would passengers who have not yet **checked in** please report immediately to **Check-in Counter** 27, and then proceed to **passport control**, and afterwards to **Gate** 30.

f You see, if you go by air, you will have a **stopover** in Nice because there is no direct flight from here to Naples until the following afternoon. But if you took the overnight train from Paris, the **fare** would be much cheaper, and you would arrive in Naples about the same time, according to this **timetable** . . .

g This is the **captain** speaking. Please assemble **on deck** at the point indicated in your **cabin**, and prepare to **abandon ship**. You will find your **life jacket** in the cabin. This is an emergency, not a **lifeboat** drill . . .

h That's right, **porter**. Put the trunk there, and the suitcases with it . . .
I'm sorry, madam, but our flight has already been called, so we have the right to jump the **queue** . . .
Here are the tickets . . . What do you mean, we have to go to the **excess baggage** counter? Don't you realise we'll miss our flight?
I'm sorry, sir, but you are ten kilos **overweight** . . .

a Why are aircraft equipped with life jackets? Where can passengers buy duty-free goods before boarding the aircraft? Why do so many people buy them?

b What would you do in this situation if you had a first-class ticket to Chester?

c What would you do if you were planning to fly to Manchester?

d What are the advantages and disadvantages of following the travel agent's advice in this situation?

e Supposing you heard this as you came into the airport. What would you do, and in what order?

f If the passenger went by air, what would he or she have to do on arriving at Nice? What could he or she do instead?

g Why do you imagine that passengers on a ship would normally take no notice of such an announcement if the captain did not make it clear that it was serious? What would you do in this situation?

h Which three people is the speaker talking to? Why is he annoyed when he speaks to the third person? Why does she insist that he must go to the excess baggage counter?

Revision

Complete the sentences, using the correct word or phrase from those you have seen above. To help you, the first letter of each word is given.

1 Sailors say 'port' and 'starboard' instead of 'left' and 'right'. Don't talk to them about 'the front' or 'the back' either, or you may be thrown overboard. You must say 'the b_____' and 'the s_____'.

2 P_____ of a_____ don't like you calling what they fly 'a plane' either, though the worst insult would be to call them 'plane drivers'.

3 The train now standing at p_____ 6 is the 9.28 e_____ train to Liverpool. P_____s with first-class tickets should note that the first-class c_____s are situated at the rear of the train.

4 He is afraid of flying, so he always asks for a w_____ s_____ next to the e_____ e_____. It wouldn't do him much good if the aircraft crashed, of course, and even the l_____ j_____s are only useful if you come down on water.

5 Let's go through p_____ c_____ as soon as we've c_____ in. Then we can go into the d_____ l_____ straightaway. The aircraft is not due to t_____ o_____ for another forty minutes so we have time to buy things in the d_____-f_____ shop.

6 All the passengers were standing on the q_____ waiting to go on b_____ the l_____ and begin their v_____ across the Atlantic.

7 I don't like sitting in my c_____ looking out at the sea through a p_____. Let's go up on d_____ and get some fresh air. If we're lucky the c_____ may invite us on to the b_____, and we can see him steering the ship.

8 How much is the f_____ to Manchester, please?
S_____ or return?
First-class return. Is there a d_____ c_____ on the train?
Just a moment. I'll look at the t_____. There isn't one on the 11.20 but there's a b_____ service if you're hungry.

SECTION TWO

Unit 10
Food, restaurants and hotels

1 Which of the following are fruits and which are vegetables?
apple banana bean cabbage carrot celery cherry lemon lettuce
marrow onion orange pea peach pear pineapple plum potato
strawberry tomato

Which is your favourite fruit, and which is your favourite vegetable?

2 Which of the following are kinds of meat and which are fish?
beef cod herring mutton pork sardine sole trout veal venison

From which of the following five animals do the kinds of meat come?
cow calf deer pig sheep

3 Match the containers in the left-hand column with the kinds of food in the right-hand column. Write the appropriate number in the right-hand column to match the letter on the left.
1 A bottle of a chocolates
2 A box of b crisps
3 A jar of c sardines
4 A packet of d milk
5 A tin of e jam

4 Match the quantities in the left hand column with the kinds of food in the right-hand column. Write the appropriate number in the right hand column to match the letter on the left.
1 A bar of a water
2 A grain of b bread
3 A loaf of c chocolate
4 A lump of d rice
5 A drop of e sugar

5 Match these traditional combinations of food, finding the correct word in the right-hand column that goes with the word in the left-hand column. Write the appropriate number in the right-hand column to match the letter on the left.
1 bacon and a biscuits
2 bread and b eggs
3 cheese and c marmalade
4 fish and d butter
5 toast and e chips

6 Which of the ways of cooking on the left seems to you most appropriate for the kind of food on the right. Match the items. Write the appropriate number in the right-hand column to match the number on the left.

1	boil	*a*	eggs and bacon
2	fry	*b*	fruit
3	grill	*c*	cabbage
4	roast	*d*	a steak
5	stew	*e*	a joint of beef

7 What actions would you normally perform in dealing with the five kinds of food listed? Match the verbs with the nouns. Write the appropriate number in the right-hand column to match the number on the left.

1	chop	*a*	a banana
2	melt	*b*	bread
3	peel	*c*	butter
4	slice	*d*	soup
5	stir	*e*	carrots

8 How would you normally serve these different kinds of liquid refreshment? Match the container with the liquid. Write the appropriate number in the right-hand column to match the letter on the left.

1	A bowl	of	*a*	beer
2	A cup	of	*b*	wine
3	A glass	of	*c*	soup
4	A mug	of	*d*	tea
5	A tankard	of	*e*	cocoa

What is a saucer for?

9 Look at this advertisement and then answer the following questions, indicating the words and phrases in the text that show your answer is correct.

SAM'S SNACK BAR
Self-service Restaurant
Our specialities
Roast beef, ham and cheese salads   Giant hamburgers
Pizzas – 12 varieties   Home-made cakes and pastries
Licensed to serve alcoholic beverages

Take-away food at bargain prices
Sandwiches   Pizzas   Fish and chips   Ice cream

---

a Are there waiters or waitresses in this restaurant?
b Can you eat both hot and cold food there?
c Is there a list of everything served?
d Could you drink beer in this restaurant?
e Why is 'take-away' food called that? Where would you eat it?

10 James and Margaret are having a dinner at a restaurant. Some restaurants have an à la carte menu with a number of different dishes at different prices, but this one has a table d'hôte menu at a fixed price, with a choice of dishes for each course. Drinks are extra.

MENU

Grapefruit
Onion soup
Prawn cocktail

Fillet of plaice
Sirloin steak
Roast lamb with mint sauce

A wide selection of desserts from the trolley

Coffee

James	What do you fancy as a starter?
Margaret	I think I'll have prawn cocktail.
James	So will I. And for the main course?
Margaret	Roast lamb, I think. How about you?
James	That looks nice, but I'd rather have a steak.
Waiter	Are you ready to order, sir?
James	Yes. Two prawn cocktails, please. After that, one roast lamb, and I'll have a steak.
Waiter	How would you like it cooked, sir?
James	Medium rare, please.
Waiter	What vegetables would you like with the lamb, madam? We have broccoli, or peas, or there's a selection.
Margaret	We'll have the selection, shall we?
James	Fine.
Waiter	Boiled potatoes, madam, or roast?
Margaret	Boiled, please.
James	And french fried for me, please.
Waiter	Very good, sir. Would you like to see the wine list?

Would you have chosen the same as James and/or Margaret? Which dish would you choose *a* as a starter; *b* as a main course? What kind of dessert would you like to follow?

11 Look at the list of people working in a hotel and decide which one is most likely to say the following:
cashier chambermaid doorman head waiter night porter porter receptionist telephonist waiter

a Would you like me to get you a taxi?
b Have you booked a table?
c Would you mind filling in this card and signing the register?
d Are you going to pay by credit card?
e Would you like to see the desserts on the trolley?
f That's all right, sir. Leave the keys with me.
g I'll take your cases and meet you upstairs.
h I'm sorry. I didn't realise you were packing. I'll come back later.
i Your room number is 223. The porter will take you up.
j Would you like an early morning call?
k There's a call from Athens for you, sir. Will you take it in your room?
l Well, you see, there's an extra charge for room service, and this figure at the bottom is Value Added Tax.

Revision

Complete the sentences, using the correct word from those you have seen above. To help you, the first letter of each word is given.

1 What did you have for breakfast?
B_____ and e_____s, t_____ and m_____, and a c_____ of coffee, with only one l_____ of sugar. I'm putting on weight.
2 A l_____of bread, three p_____s of crisps and a b_____ of milk chocolate, please.
I'm afraid we're out of milk chocolate. Would you take a b_____ of chocolates instead?
3 C_____ the meat into small pieces. P_____ the onions and s_____ them. M_____ the fat in a pan and f_____ the meat and onions until the onions are golden and the meat is tender. Meanwhile, b_____ the hot stock, and when it is ready, s_____ a few tablespoons into the meat.
4 It's cold today. I'd like a b_____ of soup to start with, and then I'll have some r_____ beef sandwiches.
Would you like a g_____ of wine with the sandwiches?
No, I'll have beer, please, in a t_____, if you have one.
5 It's s_____-s_____, which saves time. Go along that counter with your tray. Salads are their s_____. They do t_____-a_____ food as well, but that's at the other counter.
6 Would you like to have a look at the à la carte m_____, sir?
No, this will be OK. We'll have grapefruit j_____ for the s_____ and for the m_____ c_____, two fillet steaks.
How would you like them cooked?
One well done, and one m_____ r_____, please.
Thank you. Afterwards you can choose your d_____ from the t_____. The w_____ will bring it round.
7 When I checked in, the r_____ asked me to sign the r_____.
8 We ordered breakfast in bed through room service, but the c_____ came in to clean the room in the middle of it.
9 When checking out of the hotel, please settle your account with the c_____.
10 Good heavens! We've hardly got time to pack. I should have asked the n_____ p_____ for an e_____ m_____ call.

Unit 11
Farm, countryside and seaside

1 Look at the drawing of the farmyard and name each of the numbered features, using the list that follows.

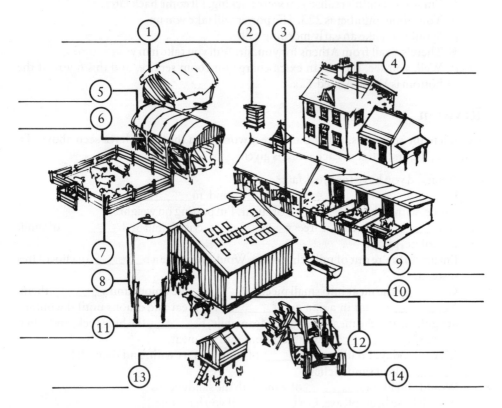

Choose from this list:
barn bee hive cowshed farmhouse hay haystack hen house plough
pigsty sheep fold silo stable tractor trough

Which of the objects are used for the following purposes?
a providing animals with water *b* pulling farm machinery *c* storing crops
d storing winter food for the animals *e* turning over the soil in fields

2 Each of the actions in the left-hand column is associated with one of the nouns in the right-hand column. Match the action to the correct noun. Write the appropriate number in the right-hand column to match the letter on the left.

1 breeding *a* the land
2 harvesting *b* cattle
3 milking *c* seeds
4 ploughing *d* cows
5 sowing *e* crops

In what season of the year in your country do farmers plough, sow and harvest?

3 Which of the following are crops, and which are trees. Which are the most common in your country?
barley beech elm fir maize oak pine rice rye wheat

4 Each of the pairs of the words listed below is related but there is a difference between them. For example, forest—wood; a forest and a wood are both places where trees grow together, but a wood is much smaller.
Define the differences between the following:
a plant – weed *b* tree – bush *c* grass – hay *d* field – meadow *e* trunk – log
f earth – clay *g* ground – soil *h* lane – path *i* plant – herb *j* root – bulb

5 Read the following text, making sure that you understand the meaning of the words in different type.

> Marc comes from a small village in the **foothills** of the Pyrenees. The village lies in a fertile **valley**, and the houses are built on the **banks** of a river and on the **slopes** of a hill. Behind there is a **range** of mountains, and last summer we set out to climb the highest **peak**. At first, it was easy. We followed the course of one of the many **streams** that form the river. Marc took a photograph of me with a **waterfall** in the background. The climb was not hard, but took longer than I expected. When we reached the **summit**, I was very tired, but the wonderful **view** we had, with the magnificent mountain **landscape** around us, and the contrasting **scenery** of the green valley below, made our effort worthwhile.

What is the countryside like near your home, or outside the city where you live?

6 Look at the drawing below, tracing the course of the River Hatch. Name each of the numbered features, using this list:
bay canal channel cove dam estuary lighthouse marsh source tributary

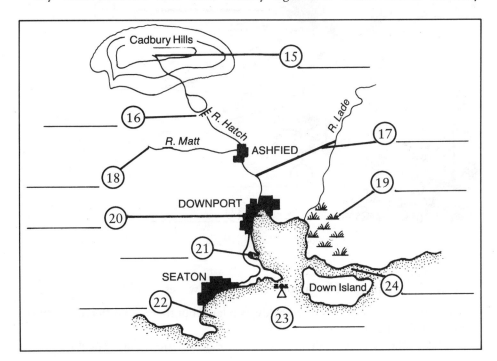

Now complete this account of the course of the River Hatch.

The _____ of the Hatch is near Linsley, in the Cadbury Hills. A _____ has been built above Ashfield, where it is joined by its _____, the Matt, and between Ashfield and Downport, where it reaches the sea, there is a _____ linking it to the Lade. The _____ of the river is a natural harbour, but Downport has developed only on the western side because of the low-lying land to the east of the mouth of the Lade; this _____ serves as a bird sanctuary. Downport is linked by road to the tourist resort of Seaton, which stands on a fine _____ protected from the wind, and not far from the road is the popular bathing place, the Fisherman's _____. Navigation into the estuary is primarily through the southern entrance, marked by a _____, rather than through the narrow _____ separating Down Island from the mainland.

Can you describe the course of a river you know well in similar terms.

7 Look at the drawing of the seashore, and identify the items listed below. Then answer the questions.

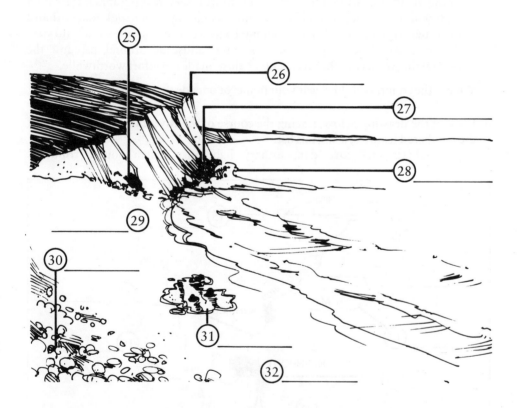

Choose from this list:
beach cave cliff pebbles pool rocks sand waves

Each of the pairs of words listed below is related but there is a difference between them. Define the differences:
a beach – sand *b* beach – shore *c* shore – coast *d* pool – pond *e* pebbles – rocks

Revision

1 Name the places where the following livestock are kept:
   a bees *b* cows *c* hens *d* horses *e* pigs *f* sheep

Complete the sentences below, using the correct word or phrase from those you have seen above. To help you, the first letter of each word is given.

2 He is in the garden pulling up the w_____s.
3 They are cutting down a tree to get l_____s for the fire.
4 We can grow all kinds of c_____s on this land because the s_____ is so rich.
5 In August, there is a festival in the village to celebrate the h_____.
6 This s_____ of the mountain is much steeper than on the eastern side.
7 The highest point of this r_____ of mountains is the p_____ of Snowdon.
8 You would not imagine that this little s_____ could be the s_____ of such a great river.
9 Before the invention of the railways, most goods were transported by water and a system of c_____s was built to link the rivers.
10 From the l_____ at the entrance of the river e_____, you have a wonderful v_____ of the whole c_____ as far as Seaton B_____.

Unit 12
Weather and climate

1 Read the late-night weather forecast given below, and then answer the questions.

Tonight will continue cold in most areas, with temperatures falling to 1 degree centigrade (34 degrees Fahrenheit) in the South and Midlands, and to zero or below freezing point in the North and Scotland. The night will be clear – a fine moonlit night in the eastern part of the country – but we can expect some snow to fall on high ground in Wales and the West, and there will be widespread frost overnight with the risk of early morning fog patches, and mist in coastal districts.

Turning to tomorrow's chart, the outlook is similar for the eastern half of the country, in general fine and dry, but there will be some snow, turning to sleet as temperatures rise during the day, in Yorkshire and the North-east. During the day, a warmer westerly airstream will enter Wales and the South-west, and temperatures there will go up to 7 degrees centigrade (46 degrees Fahrenheit). The general tendancy will be drizzle and some light rain in the West, but take an umbrella because some outbreaks of heavier rain are likely, and there could even be some isolated thunderstorms.

Looking forward to Tuesday, the warmer weather will spread eastward across the country, with showers but also some sunny intervals.

a What is freezing point?
b Why would you expect snow if you lived in the Welsh mountains?
c Why would you need to drive carefully the following morning?
d Why would it be dangerous to play football in the morning?
e What is the difference between snow and sleet? What does sleet become if the temperature rises?
f What sort of rain is drizzle?
g Why would it be wise to take an umbrella tomorrow if you lived in the West?
h Would you take an umbrella on Tuesday? Why/Why not?

2 Britain seldom experiences extreme weather conditions. Which of the eight areas of the world listed do you associate with the following?
an avalanche drought an earthquake floods a hurricane a snowstorm
a typhoon a volcanic eruption
Antarctica Bangladesh California Florida northern Africa Sicily
the South China Sea Switzerland

3 Study the chart of the weather conditions in different cities of the world. The upper line of figures for each city refers to the average temperature (°C); the lower line refers to rainfall (ml.). The last column on the right indicates the average temperature and the total rainfall for a year.

a Where would you describe the climate as 'hot all year round'?
b Which cities have 'a rainy season', and when does it occur?
c Which cities have winters you would describe as: mild (temperate, not cold), hot and dry, bright and refreshing (cold and dry), damp (cool and wet), bitterly cold?

52

	Winter Jan.	Feb.	Spring Mar.	Apr.	May	Summer Jun.	Jul.	Aug.	Autumn Sept.	Oct.	Nov.	Winter Dec.	
Athens	9	10	11	15	19	24	27	26	23	19	14	11	17
	53	43	30	23	20	18	8	13	18	41	66	66	394
Bombay	24	24	26	28	30	29	27	27	27	28	27	25	27
	3	–	3	–	18	523	693	406	300	61	10	–	2017
Madrid	5	7	9	12	16	21	25	25	20	13	8	5	14
	33	33	41	41	43	33	10	13	38	46	51	41	422
Mexico City	12	14	16	17	18	18	17	17	16	15	14	12	16
	5	5	15	15	48	99	104	119	104	46	13	5	587
Moscow	−11	−9	−4	3	12	16	18	16	10	4	−3	−8	4
	33	30	36	36	46	66	81	79	53	53	46	41	599
Peking	−5	−2	5	14	20	25	26	25	20	13	4	−3	12
	3	5	5	15	36	76	239	160	66	15	8	3	632

d When do you think would be the most pleasant time of year to visit each city? It depends on what sort of weather you like yourself.

e Which cities have the greatest extremes of climate, and which cities have the most temperate climate, with few extremes of any kind?

Revision

Complete the passage below, using the correct word or phrase from those you have seen above. To help you, the first letter of each word is given.

WEATHER FORECAST

General situation: A SW airstream will extend across the country, gradually bringing w_____ weather. S_____ in all areas, with h_____ rain in some places.

   London, SE, E Anglia, Channel Islands: C_____, rain, becoming heavier during the day. W_____ S or SW, moderate or fresh. Temp. 10–11°C.

   Central, E: Beginning d_____ and b_____. Afternoon s_____. Wind S, m_____. Temp 8–10°C.

   SW, NW England, Wales, Isle of Man: Beginning moist, with early morning d_____. M_____ in coastal d_____, and risk of f_____ patches. O_____ of heavier rain during the morning. Temp. rising to 12–14°C. F_____ evening, d_____, as clouds move eastward.

   W Scotland, N Ireland: Overnight f_____, sunny i_____ during the morning, but rain spreading during the afternoon, becoming s_____ as temperatures fall. S_____ on high ground. Wind f_____ or strong. Temp 4–8°C.

   E Scotland: Heavy frost o_____ and near f_____ temperatures. C_____, mainly d_____, but some local s_____ showers later. Temp 0–4°C.

   Further o_____: Changeable with r_____ or s_____. S_____ or s_____ over N hills. Near normal t_____.

Unit 13
Letters and telephone calls

1 Jane Smith is cooking the lunch for her nine-year-old son, Stephen, when the door-bell rings. Read the dialogue, making sure that you understand the meaning of all the words in different type, and then answer the questions.

Jane	Oh, there's the door. Stephen, will you answer it?
Stephen	It's the postman, Mum. You've got to **sign** for a letter because it's a **recorded delivery**.
Jane	(*at the door*) Good morning, what do I have to do?
Postman	If you'd just put your **signature** here on the **dotted line** on the **form**, please. Actually, I had to ring anyway, because this **packet** wouldn't go through the **letter box**. And there's one other thing. I'm afraid there's insufficient **postage** on this letter. 10p extra to pay.
Jane	All right. Here you are. It's from Aunt Ethel. I recognise the **handwriting**. She never puts enough stamps on. Thank you, goodbye.
Stephen	What's that blue **envelope**, Mum?
Jane	That's an air letter. It's from your Uncle Alec in Canada. Now what else have we got here? A **postcard** from Mrs Binks in Devon. Hm, she's enjoying her holiday, but the weather's awful. And a **recorded** letter for your Dad. I wonder what this is. This packet must be a piece of cousin Sarah's wedding cake, all **wrapped up** in silver paper, and **tied** with pretty **string**. She certainly sent a big slice. No wonder it wouldn't go through the letter box. Hey, this letter's got the wrong **address** on it. Run after the postman, and give it back to him.
Stephen	But it says Mr K R Smith, Mum.
Jane	Yes, but Daddy's **initials** are K L, and this is addressed to 34 Thorn Crescent, not 17 Woodfield Avenue. Quick! There's the postman over there, talking to Mrs Sugden. Hm, and what's this? (*she tears open an envelope*) Oh, the **reminder** to pay the TV **licence**, of course. I meant to go round to the **post office** last week . . .

a Do you know how much the postage is from your country to Britain?
b Why do people use air letters for correspondence abroad?
c And why do they ask for recorded delivery?
d Is your handwriting easy to read? Is your signature easily recognised? Could people copy it easily?
e Why do you think the postman calls what he delivers a packet? What do you need to wrap up a parcel? Describe what you do, using these words: **Sellotape**, **string**, **scissors**.
f Do you have to fill in a form to send a parcel in your country? Do you have to sign your name?
g What do you think is the difference between a letter box and a postbox? What colour are the postboxes in your country? Do you know what colour they are in Britain?
h Do you need a licence to watch television in your country? Do you need one for anything else – to keep a dog, for example?

2 Read the notice carefully and compare it with the instructions in your country. Are the procedures and the tones (the sounds) the same? Answer the questions.

COIN OPERATED PAYPHONES

When you make a call
1 First check the code, if any, and the number in the telephone directory.
2 Lift the handset and listen for the dial tone.
3 Insert the coins until the credit indicator stops flashing.
4 Key the number and wait for connection.
5 Insert further coins as necessary.
6 Wholly unused coins will be returned at the end of the call, but no change will be given for partially used coins.
7 To make a second call using unexpired credit do not hang up, but press the continuation button on the handset hook to regain the dial tone.

Caution: If there is no display, or the display indicates '999 calls only', normal telephone service is not available and no money should be inserted.

TONES

Dial tone
A continuous purring or high-pitched hum.

Ringing tone
A repeated burr – burr sound.

Engaged (busy) tone
A repeated single note.

Number unobtainable
A continuous steady note. This means that the number is out of order or currently not in use, or an incorrect dialling code has been used.

If you were trying to make a call from a payphone in Britain, what would you do in the following circumstances?
a You could not remember the number of the person you wanted to ring.
b He or she lived in another town and you could not remember the code.
c You lifted the handset and heard the dial tone.
d You wanted to make another call and use the money you had already put in?
e The display read '999' calls only?
f You heard a steady note?
g You heard the engaged tone?

3 Paul and Sally are at the airport in Madrid. They have just heard that their flight to London will be delayed for three hours, so they decide to ring Paul's partner, Barry, to tell him about the delay.

Sally	Here's a payphone that seems to be working. I can hear the **dial tone**. The **code** for England is 07 44, I think, and then dial the number.
Paul	Here we go then. 07, wait for the international tone, 44, 1 – 263 5288. Oh dear! The line's **engaged**.
Sally	Never mind. We've got plenty of time.
Paul	I'll **dial** again. Now we're **through**.
Voice	Hello.
Paul	(*presses the button*) Hello, could I speak to Barry Cranfield, please.
Voice	It's a very **bad line**. Did you say Gary? We haven't got any Gary here, I'm afraid.
Paul	No, BARRY. Mr Barry Cranfield. Is that Cranfield Electric?
Voice	No, dear, this is the Bunny Rabbit Club. Can I help you?
Paul	I don't think so. Sorry, I must have **dialled the wrong number**. (*replaces the handset*) Let's try again. Oh, good, third time lucky.
2nd voice	Hello, Cranfield Electric.
Paul	Could I speak to Barry Cranfield, please?
2nd voice	**Hold the line**, please. I'm just putting you through.
Paul	(*after some seconds*) Have you got any more coins, darling? Hello? Hello? Put them in the **coin slot**, will you?
2nd voice	I'm still trying to **connect** you.
Paul	Could you hurry, please? I'm speaking from the airport in Madrid, you see.
2nd voice	**You're through** now, sir.
3rd voice	Mr Cranfield's secretary speaking. Can I help you?
Paul	Yes, I'd like to speak to Mr Cranfield, please, Joy. This is Paul Summers.
3rd voice	Oh, hello, Mr Summers. Mr Cranfield's gone out, I'm afraid. Can I **take a message**?
Paul	Yes, please. Would you tell him that my wife and I are held up in Madrid? Our flight's delayed, so we now expect to get in about four o'clock. Ah, now we've run out of money, and **the line's gone dead**. Still, I think she got the message.

a How does Sally know the payphone is working?
b Why doesn't Paul get through the first time he dials the number?
c How does he know he is through?
d Why does the first voice think he said 'Gary'?
e Why can't he speak to his partner after the second call?
f How else could you say 'Hold the line'?
g Why does Sally have to put some more money in the coin slot?
h What is the telephonist trying to do meanwhile?
i How does Paul eventually contact Barry?
j Why is he not quite sure that his message has been received, and what is the reason for this?

Revision

Complete the sentences, using the correct word or phrase from those you have seen above. To help you, the first letter of each word is given.

1 You have to s_____ when the postman brings r_____ l_____.

2 Where do I put my s_____?
   On the d_____ l_____ at the bottom of the f_____. Hey, you've signed
   X Y Z Brown. They can't be your i_____s.
   Oh, yes they are. My name is Xanthe Yolande Zoe.

3 Look at the h_____ on this e_____, Bill. I can hardly read the a_____.
   How do they expect the P_____ O_____ to d_____ the m_____ when
   they write so badly?

4 If you do not hear the d_____ t_____ when you pick up the telephone, it may
   be out of o_____. Replace the h_____, and try again. If you are still unable
   to obtain the l_____, please contact the telephone service from the nearest
   p_____. No charge will be made for your call.

5 I had a terrible time getting through to you. First the number was e_____. Then
   I stupidly d_____ the w_____ number. Finally, your telephonist made me
   h_____ the line for so long while she was trying to c_____ me that I ran out
   of change and the line went d_____.

Unit 14
Records, radio and television

1 Look at the picture of the record player and name each of the numbered features, using the list that follows:

Choose from this list:
amplifier arm loudspeakers record record player stylus turntable

Describe how you would put a record on manually.
On the amplifier there are four knobs; match the name of the knob in the left-hand column to its purpose on the right. Write the appropriate number in the right-hand column to match the letter on the left.

1 bass control   *a* keeps the sound even
2 sound balance control   *b* emphasises the higher notes
3 treble control   *c* enables you to make the sound louder or softer
4 volume control   *d* emphasises the lower notes

2 Read the following text and then answer the questions.

This is the World Service of the BBC, broadcasting from London. **Listeners** in southern Europe should **tune** to one of the following **frequencies** on the **short waveband** in order to continue listening to this **programme** – 7.32 megahertz, 9.67 megahertz or 11.71 megahertz.

Your radio has four knobs, marked **tone control, tuner, waveband control** and **volume control**.
Which one would you adjust
a to switch from the short wave to the long wave
b to find the right frequency, for example, 7.32 megahertz
c to raise the level of the sound
d to get clearer reception?

Suppose you wanted to listen to a programme on the World Service, but at first you got poor reception. Describe what you would do.

3 Read the following text, making sure you understand the meaning of all the words in different type.

> Well, it's Ken Plugg, your favourite **disc jockey**, here again on Radio 19 with this week's **Hit Parade**. Just coming in at number 20 on the **charts** is the hit **tune** from the Dumbos' latest **album**, 'Rock 'n' Roll Party'. You've heard it in the **disco** already, and you're going to hear it on the radio all summer. The Dumbos are a group with their own unique **rhythm**, an unmistakable **beat** from Tom Hammer on the drums that will drive you crazy! Wayne Dumbo himself is at the **mike**, Craig Clodd and Jacko Mumble are on electric guitars . . .
> . . . And now just listen to the **applause** that greeted Australian **ballad** singer Charlene Bruce from all the **fans** at the Stockwell **Folk Festival**. She provides her own **accompaniment**. The **close-harmony vocal backing** is by the Boo-Boo Trio . . .

Do you listen to programmes like this? Do you buy records because they are recommended by disc jockeys, you see their names in the charts, or you hear them in a disco?

Do you prefer groups or individual singers?

What sort of music do you prefer: classical, pop, soul, country and western, jazz, rock 'n' roll, folk songs?

4 Study the programmes on the two channels below.

VIEWERS' GUIDE FOR EVENING TV

Channel 5

6.00	Newsreel.
6.20	The weather with Bert Spratt.
6.30	'Peoples of the World'. The fourth in the series. Script: Janet Pearce.
7.30	'Paradise Street' Long-running serial.
8.15	'Next Question', a quiz show, presented by Alan Grundy.
9.00	News and weather.
9.30	Interview. Jill Long interviews the Minister of Health.
10.30	Sports Hour. Highlights of the England v Spain game: commentator, Peter Groves.
11.30	Late-night news.

Southward

6.00	South News, read by Paul Drake. Followed by regional weather forecast.
6.15	'Goofy'. Cartoons.
6.30	'Guess the Tune' the popular panel game. Chairman: Hugh Duffy.
7.30	'Night of the Stars' Musical show, compèred by Brian Langley (repeat)
9.00	'War and Peace' (Episode 4) with Michael Everett, Natasha Brown. Adapted by June Clough
10.00	News Desk, presented by Jason Bartlett and Fiona Hill.
10.30	'The Changing Landscape'. Documentary.
11.15	The late-night film. 'M' introduced by Phyllis Dell.
1.00	Close down.

Decide which programmes you would like to see. Make sure that you understand what each programme consists of, and what sort of job the different people mentioned do.

Make sure that you understand what each programme consists of, and what sort of job the different people mentioned do.

Would you have any arguments at home with other members of the family who would like to see something different? Which choice of programmes would cause the arguments?

Revision

Complete the text, using the words and phrases you have seen above, but note that in some cases the word may be a little different – for example, 'interviewer' instead of 'interview'. To help you, the first letter of each word is given.

TONIGHT'S VIEWING by Stephen Harris

Not a very inspiring evening for v_____ tonight, but Channel 5's s_____ on peoples of the world, immediately after the w_____ f_____, is worth watching, with an intelligent s_____ by Janet Pearce. Music lovers, however, will t_____ in to 'Guess the Tune', a p_____ g_____ with a first-class c_____ in Hugh Duffy that is always interesting. Only addicts can still face the interminable s_____, 'Paradise Street', but c_____ Brian Langley livens up the musical show on Southward, if you haven't seen it already. 'Next Question' is the kind of silly q_____ s_____ I can't stand, and Alan Grundy, the p_____, always looks as if he felt the same way. Jill Long is the most aggressive i_____ on TV and the Minister will no doubt be concerned about his own health, but I have been enchanted by Natasha Brown in previous e_____s of 'War and Peace', and June Clough's skilful a_____ deserves high praise. I will not watch 'News Desk', because clever p_____s, Jason Bartlett and Fiona Hill, are bound to tell me the result of the football match on the other c_____ at 10.30 and spoil it and the recorded h_____, but I will turn the sound off during the game so as not to hear c_____ Peter Groves' banal remarks and artificial excitement. Afterwards, I will watch 'M', the classic thriller, but unfortunately I will have to do without Phyllis Dell's excellent i_____.

Unit 15
Newspapers

1 A large number of people, doing different jobs, are employed in producing and selling newspapers every day. Match the name of the job in the left-hand column to the correct definition of the work the people do. Write the appropriate number in the right-hand column to match the letter on the left.

1 Cartoonist	*a*	comments on new books
2 City Editor	*b*	commissions special articles
3 Our Own Correspondent	*c*	does humorous drawings
4 Critic	*d*	edits articles sent in by reporters
5 Editor	*e*	is responsible for the content and policy of the newspaper
6 Features Editor		
7 Freelance journalist	*f*	is responsible for financial news
8 Gossip columnist	*g*	is sent to report on events
9 Leader writer	*h*	owns the newspaper
10 Newsagent	*i*	sells newspapers in a shop
11 News vendor	*j*	sells newspapers in the street
12 Proprietor	*k*	represents a particular newspaper in one place (e.g. a foreign capital)
13 Reporter		
14 Reviewer	*l*	submits articles to different newspapers
15 Subeditor	*m*	writes editorials
	n	writes about new films, plays, etc.
	o	writes about the social life of well-known people

2 The subeditor is responsible for writing the headlines for articles. On which pages of the newspaper would you expect to find the following headlines?
the front page (main news)   the editorial page   the fashion page   the sports page
the gossip column   the travel page   the situations vacant column   the City page
the features page   the review page

Welcome to the Isle of Wight

Prime Minister resigns

O'Toole murders Macbeth

Coe breaks world record

Soft colours this summer

Pope to meet Falcon Crest star

How I saved the Olympic Games

Will Distillers take-over bid succeed?

The President and his critics

Calling all graduates

3 Apart from news, newspapers also contain many other features:
advertisements   announcements of births, marriages and deaths
crossword puzzles   horoscopes   letters from readers
obituaries of famous people who have died   TV and radio programmes
weather forecasts   classified advertisements (which may be personal or
advertise jobs, houses or cars for sale, objects wanted, etc.)

The twelve newspaper extracts below come from each of the categories listed
above. Decide where each extract comes from.

1. **6.30** The Money Programme with Brian Wildlake and Valerie Singleton.

2. All other areas. Cloudy some bright intervals. Isolated showers. Winds, light to variable.

3. Much of Donald Craig's article on London (January 18) was helpful and well-informed. However, it contained some errors and omissions.

4. The footballer who took only fifty per cent (4,4).

5. B. I waited for you all Thursday evening and all Friday evening, too. Where are you? What do you think I am, a bus stop? Please ring and explain. I love you in spite of everything. H.

6. **BMW 525 Auto 82.** 1 owner. Every extra, including leather. Immaculate condition. £5,885.

7. Lt Col Hugh Truscott, VC, who died yesterday at his home in Sussex, was a veteran of two world wars. Colonel Truscott, who was 87, . . .

8. *Old violins, cellos and other musical instruments urgently required. Best prices. Mayer, 86 Goldhawk Road, W37 or ring 01 246 8041.*

9. *Take your children to Europe this year! Self-drive, family holidays on over 100 superb camping sites in 15 different countries!*

10. Avoid arguments with people at home and at work. You are likely to be bad-tempered, but cheer up! You could be in line for an unexpected windfall.

11. **A** beautiful fully-furnished villa. 4 double bedrooms, fitted wardrobes. Lounge, stone-built fireplace. Large, fully-fitted kitchen.

12. SPRATT and PONSONBY-SMYTHE Kevin Gary to Fiona Laetitia, at St Ethelred's, Bexhill.

Revision

Colin Hunter is a young reporter on a local newspaper, *The Farley Argus*. Read this account of his experience after working there for a few months. Complete the passage, using the correct word or phrase from those you have seen above. To help you, the first letter of each word is given.

The life of a young r_____ on a local newspaper is not easy. When you start, you imagine yourself as a l_____ w_____, commenting on world affairs so intelligently that the paper receives hundreds of r_____s' letters congratulating you on the e_____. In fact, you have to be everything, without being anyone. On Wednesdays, I do the h_____s, usually saying something nice about my sign and my girlfriend's. On Thursdays, I write the g_____ c_____, though in my case it only concerns the Mayor and his friends. On Fridays, I am book r_____, even though most of our readers only read the s_____ pages of the *Argus*, and on Saturdays, I write those, too. I watch football matches in the pouring rain and think of wonderful h_____s, but the s_____-e_____ changes them, and often changes the result, too. I am also film c_____ but I can't criticise the films because the p_____ of the *Argus* also owns the local cinema. If I could draw, I expect they would make me the c_____! The only other j_____ on our staff is Sally. She does the woman's page, and also the f_____s page, which she copies out of the colour supplements in the national Sunday papers. The most important person in the office is Jack, the advertising manager. As he says: 'All these classified a_____s, the a_____s of births and marriages and the situations v_____ c_____ for people looking for jobs and so on, pay for the rubbish you write.' I hope that one day I will be able to write his o_____.

Unit 16
Plays, films and opera

1 The table given below is incomplete in some places. Find the correct words from the list underneath to fill the gaps.

Plays	Films	Opera
_____	cinema	opera house
stage	_____	stage
play (text)	_____	music, libretto (words)
dramatist or playwright	screenwriter	_____, librettist
actor	actor	_____
actress	actress	
supporting cast	supporting cast	_____
	extras	
understudy	_____	understudy
director	director	director (opera)
		_____ (orchestra)
act	scene	act
scene		scene
speech (1 character)	speech	_____ (1 singer)
dialogue (2 characters)	dialogue	_____ (2 singers)
_____	scene before titles	_____

Choose from this list:
aria chorus composer conductor duet overture prologue screenplay set singer stand-in takes theatre

2 Match the people in the left-hand column to the appropriate job in the theatre on the right. Write the appropriate number in the right-hand column to match the letter on the left.

1 a choreographer   *a* puts make-up on the actors' faces
2 a costume designer   *b* designs the scenery on the stage
3 a prompter   *c* looks after everything on stage during the performance
4 a make-up artist   *d* designs the clothes the actors wear
5 a set designer   *e* tells the actors their lines when they forget
6 a stage hand   *f* is responsible for dances on the stage
7 a stage manager   *g* shows the audience to their seats
8 an usher   *h* helps the stage manager, moves scenery

3 Read the dialogue and look at the diagram of the theatre. Gerry is telephoning the box office because he wants to buy two tickets for the first performance of a new play

Gerry Hello, Princess Theatre? Have you got two tickets for *Party Manners* next Wednesday?

Voice There aren't many left, I'm afraid. It's the **first night**, you see. I can give you two in the **balcony**, but you won't get a very good view. The **dress circle**

and the **upper circle** are completely booked up. I don't suppose you'd like a **box**, just for two.

Gerry Well, no. Is there anything in the **stalls**?

Voice Wait a minute. Yes, you're lucky. I've got two stalls, **Row** K, 7 and 8. They've just been returned. Will you take those? They're ten pounds each.

Gerry Oh er, yes, OK.

Voice You can pick them up from the **box office** in the **foyer** at any time up to half an hour before the performance. What name is it, please?

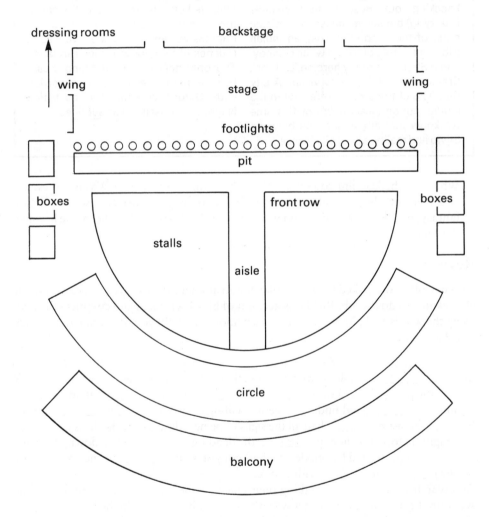

Which do you think are the most expensive seats, and which are the least expensive? Why is that?

Where do the orchestra sit in the theatre?

Where do the actors come from and go to when they make **entrances** and **exits**?

Have you ever been in a modern or ancient theatre that was different from this? What differences were there?

Why do you think **footlights** are called that, and what are they for?

When you go to the theatre, what do you do during the **interval** between the acts of the play?

4 Read these two film reviews of the feature films being shown in Farley this week, making sure that you understand the meaning of all the words underlined.

This week at the cinema

Plaza *Boot Hill* (director: Silvio Stilton) (Western). Silvio Stilton takes a rest from killing men like flies (*Bimbo*) and knocking out Russian heavyweights (*Socky VI*) but still manages to eliminate most of the supporting cast, an Indian tribe, in the role of a pure white cowboy. Tania Shore is a pretty heroine, and Jack Branston a suitably nasty villain. A pity that 90% of the scenes were shot in the studio, not on location, but by this time we know that any connection between Silvio and reality is just coincidence.

Palace *Pale Moon* (director: Toshiro Nagasawa) (epic). Nagasawa's latest three-hour saga was reverently reviewed after its London première. In the part of the samurai hero, Isao Fujikura is impressive, and there are even some touches of humour in his interpretation. The only defect is the dubbing. I can't believe in mediaeval Japanese warriors with Oxford accents. The next time Nagasawa must insist on subtitles.

What was the last film you saw, either in the cinema or on TV? Was it a Western, an adventure film, a thriller, a horror film, a comedy, a musical, a science-fiction fantasy, or a detective film? Who were the stars? Who played the hero, the heroine, the villain?

Revision

Adrian Collins was asked to direct a play for an amateur theatre group because no one else wanted to do the job. Read this account of his experiences and complete the text, using the words and phrases you have seen above. To help you, the first letter of each word is given.

The d_____ of a group of amateur a_____s has a difficult job. First, he has to find a c_____ capable of working together. It is easy enough to persuade people to take the p_____s of the h_____, h_____ and v_____, but no one wants a minor r_____, and finding someone willing to be s_____ m_____ is even harder. Our last p_____ had all the signs of being a disaster. At the dress r_____, the night before the first p_____, the leading a_____ fell down, tore her c_____ and twisted her ankle. We had not got an u_____, so she had to go on on the f_____ n_____ with a stick.
As I watched the a_____ taking their places in the s_____s before the curtain went up, I feared the worst but it was worse than I had feared. In the first a_____, the hero forgot his l_____s, couldn't hear the p_____, and made an e_____ into the w_____s to find out what he had to say next. The actor on s_____ with him didn't notice, and went on with his next s_____, turning it into a s_____.
The heroine was wearing a long dress because of her twisted ankle. She got too close to the f_____, saw smoke rising from her feet, screamed and fainted, just as the villain, making his e_____, came on and tripped over her.
During the i_____, my wife, who was helping out by acting as an u_____, showing people to their seats, said: 'Don't worry! They love it. A man in the second r_____ just said to me: "I didn't realise this was a c_____. I haven't laughed so much for years".'

Unit 17
Health

1 Study the examples of the words printed in different type and the explanations given. The right word to use depends on usage rather than on a definition in most cases. Then answer the questions below.

> I don't feel very **well**./I feel **ill**. (Stage of health.)
> He's recovering from a serious **illness**. (Period of time when one is **ill**, or the cause of being **ill**.)
> Oh dear, I feel **sick**. (I'm going to vomit/be sick.)
> I'm going to visit a **sick** child.
> He felt **ill**, so he reported **sick**/went on **sick leave**.
> When people are **ill**, the government pay **sickness** benefit.
> Cholera is an **infectious disease**. (A condition caused by an infection or an unnatural growth.)
> Many **diseases** are **contagious**. (Other people catch diseases from a person who is ill.)
> He suffered serious **injuries**./He was badly **injured** in a car accident.
> He was shot in the bank robbery but fortunately he only suffered a **flesh wound**/ was not badly **wounded**.
> The **wound** will **heal** more quickly if you let the air get to it, but there is a risk of **infection**/of it becoming **infected**.
> A **headache, toothache, earache, backache, stomachache**.
> A **pain** in the chest, a pain in my shoulder, etc.
> My shoulder **hurts**. He was seriously **hurt/injured** in an accident.
> Take your medicine. It won't **hurt** you/**harm** you/do you any **harm**.

Choose the correct word from the choices given. Only one word is correct.

a You shouldn't worry so much, you'll make yourself ill/sick.
b We do not normally allow employees time off to look after ill/sick relatives except in cases of great hardship.
c He has completely recovered but still looks weak after his long illness/sickness.
d The principal cause of death in this country is heart illness/disease.
e He was injured/wounded in the match against Arsenal last week and will not be able to play against Liverpool on Saturday.
f You must give your diseases/wounds time to heal.
g If you have a headache/pain in the head, take some aspirin.
h It's a good dog. It won't do you any harm/hurt.

2 The symptoms of an illness are the signs that indicate to doctors what a patient is suffering from. Match the symptoms in the left-hand column with the illness on the right. In some cases, more than one symptom may be evident, or a symptom may suggest more than one kind of illness. Write the appropriate number or numbers in the right-hand column to match the letter on the left.

1	a cough, nose running, sneezing	*a*	anaemia
2	dizziness, shivering, a headache	*b*	the common cold
3	fainting, double vision	*c*	food poisoning
4	high fever, high temperature	*d*	'flu (influenza)
5	headache, sickness	*e*	high blood pressure
6	rapid heart beat, out of breath	*f*	measles
7	sickness, stomachache, vomiting	*g*	migraine
8	sore throat, swelling in throat	*h*	mumps
9	spots	*i*	pneumonia
10	swelling under the ears	*j*	rheumatism
11	stiff joints	*k*	shock (mental); a blow (physical)
12	weak pulse rate, fainting	*l*	tonsilitis

3 In each of the situations listed below, the doctor or dentist is telling a child's mother what he or she is going to do to cure the trouble. Note the words printed in different type, and make sure that you understand them. Then decide which advice refers to which situation.

a Sally is in bed with a heavy cold and temperature. *b* Johnny has been stung by a bee. *c* Alan has cut his forehead badly. *d* Paula has broken her leg. *e* Mark has broken his arm. *f* Laura is very pale and anaemic. *g* James has a bad tooth. *h* Sandra has pulled a muscle.

1 Obviously, she'll have to go to hospital for an **X-ray**. With luck, it is a clean break, and young **bones set** quickly, but she'll have to have it in **plaster** for a time; she can go to school though, but naturally she'll have to go round on **crutches** until the plaster comes off.

2 I'll give you a **diet** sheet that she must follow, but apart from that I'd better give her these **vitamin pills**. She must take the tablets three times a day after meals.

3 You can get this **ointment** from the chemist's. I'll write out the **prescription** for you. Rub it gently into the **skin** every night before she goes to bed. Some people recommend **sprays** for this kind of thing, but my view is that the ointment gives more **relief**.

4 It's nothing serious. But this **medicine** will be better than the patent **cough mixtures** and **syrups** they sell in the chemist's. If she has a headache as well, give her half an **aspirin**.

5 I'm afraid this is going to hurt, but I'll give him an **injection** which will **dull the pain**. It may **ache** afterwards and you can give him an aspirin if that is the case.

6 That is nasty. I'm going to clean the **wound** with **antiseptic**, and it may **sting**. Now, here's the **cotton wool**. We'll just put a little antiseptic on it. Well done, that's a brave boy. Now we'll protect it from the air and put a **bandage** over it, and you'll look like a little soldier after a battle.

7 There's quite a lot of **swelling**, but I see you've taken the **sting** out. He must take these tablets to reduce the **inflammation**, but be very careful not to exceed the **dose**, not more than two a day, every twelve hours, for three days.

8 Once the **plaster** comes off, he'll still have to have it in a **sling** for a time to rest it.

4 Study the following, making sure that you understand the meaning of the words in different type. Decide where you would be likely to hear the statements.
   a a doctor's surgery   *b* the casualty department in a hospital   *c* at the hospital information desk

What is the situation? Describe what has probably happened.

1 I'll **take your temperature**. Just rest the **thermometer** under your tongue and keep it still. Afterwards, I'll give you a general **check-up**. But I think you're quite healthy. It's just a matter of your being **overweight** and not getting enough exercise. You mustn't start thinking that you're an **invalid**.

2 We're happy to say that the **operation** has been a complete success, and the **patient** is now **out of danger**. It won't be possible for you to see her yet because she won't be fully conscious until the effects of the **anaesthetic** have **worn off**, but I'll be able to give you more information this evening. I can tell you then which **ward** she is in and give you details of **visiting hours**.

3 I've told you before that if you continue to work such long hours with that degree of **stress**, you'll end up by having a **nervous breakdown**. I'm not going to **prescribe tranquillisers**, because you'd become dependent on them and then you'd need **pep pills** to give you **energy**. The **remedy** is in your own hands. You must **relax**, or better still, take a week's holiday and get away from the **tensions** at work which produce all this **stress and strain** and give you these **fits of depression**.

4 The **skin's** hardly broken. It's only a **scratch**. But you must have had a terrible **bump** on your head when you banged into the windscreen, and you'll have a monumental **bruise** to prove it. Take this **lotion** and apply it gently; that will bring the bruise out. Perhaps you'd better lie down for a few minutes, but fortunately there's no need to keep you in, and you can go home once you've got over the **shock**.

5 We'll try an alternative **course of treatment**, but it might be a good idea if I got the **nurse** to make an **appointment** for you to see a **specialist**. A friend of mine's a **consultant** at St. Mary's, and he may advise your going into hospital just for a few days **under observation**.

6 This is an **emergency**. The **surgeon** is already waiting in the **operating theatre**. As soon as the **ambulance** arrives, tell them to bring the patient straight through here, and then we'll wheel him into the theatre.

Revision

Complete the sentences, using the correct word or phrase from those you have seen above. To help you, the first letter of each word is given.

1 It doesn't do you any h_____ to take aspirins if you have a h_____, provided you don't exceed the d_____ indicated on the packet, but you shouldn't take antibiotics without a p_____ from the doctor.

2 He is running a f_____, with a t_____ of over 40°. Look at the t_____, and you can see for yourself.

3 In the old days a lot of soldiers who were w_____ in battle died because the w_____ became i_____.

4 I feel s_____. I shouldn't have eaten so much.
   You should be more careful. You've only just recovered from a serious i_____.

5 A p_____ has just been admitted to the h_____ suffering from a rare tropical d_____. He is being kept in isolation, as it is c_____.

6 What s_____s have you noticed?
   My j_____ are always stiff when I wake up, and sometimes I have b_____ and p_____s in my legs. I've got a s_____ throat too, but I don't suppose that's connected.
   Let me see. Yes, some i_____ in your throat, and a little s_____ on both sides of the jaw. That's a touch of t_____. Get the chemist to make this m_____ I'm going to p_____, and you could also use a throat s_____. There isn't really a c_____ for the other problem, which is r_____, but if you rub this o_____ in every night, you'll get some r_____. Otherwise, you could try and heat t_____.

7 One of my brothers is a c_____ at the County H_____, and another is a heart s_____ in London. My husband's a s_____. He's been very busy recently, because there have been a lot of accidents. He spent most of yesterday in the o_____ t_____.
   How did you meet him?
   I was a n_____ in one of the w_____s a t the hospital.

8 You must be bored, lying here with a broken leg. When are they going to take the p_____ off?
   Next week, but I'll still have to go round on c_____s for a while after that.

9 Is there anything seriously wrong with him?
   No, he's not very i_____, but he's a bit worried about his blood p_____, so he's made an a_____ with the d_____ to have a c_____-u_____.

10 He's got t_____, but he hates going to the d_____'s. When he was a child they never gave you an i_____ for a filling, and he's never forgotten the p_____ he endured.

11 He gets these terrible f_____s of d_____ because things are going so badly at work. If he's not careful, he'll have a n_____ b_____.

12 Fortunately, we haven't had any serious accidents at the school, just the usual cuts and b_____s when children fall down. But we keep a stock of a_____ to clean the w_____, and b_____s to bind them and keep out i_____.

Unit 18
Education

1 Students in Great Britain can take public examinations known as General Certificate of Secondary Education (GCSE) and Advanced ('A') level. Those who want to go to university usually take from 5–7 subjects for GCSE at 16, and three subjects at 'A' level when they are 18. In order to enter a university or polytechnic in Britain, you are expected to have two or three 'A' levels with good marks. The only subject that is compulsory for university entrance is English at GCSE, but Mathematics is often required.

Look at the chart below, which shows the ten most popular subjects with boys and girls in Britain at GCSE and 'A' level. Then answer the questions that follow.

GCSE		'A' level	
Boys	**Girls**	**Boys**	**Girls**
English	English	Mathematics	English
Mathematics	Mathematics	Physics	Biology
Physics	Biology	Chemistry	History
Geography	English Literature	Economics	Mathematics
English Literature	French	General Studies	General Studies
Chemistry	Geography	Geography	French
Biology	Art and Design	English	Chemistry
History	History	Biology	Economics
French	Chemistry	History	Art
Art and Design	Physics	Art	Geography

Which subjects would you take at 'A' level if you wanted to be the following?
'arts subjects'? Do you notice any preferences among boys and girls for one or the other?
What other subjects would you expect to find in the school curriculum? (e.g. other modern languages, ancient languages, religious or civic studies, other arts subjects)

Which three subjects would you take at 'A' level if you wanted to be the following?
a a doctor *b* an economist *c* an interpreter *d* a journalist *e* an engineer
f an actor *g* a priest *h* a naturalist *i* a painter *j* a businessman
Note that they would not necessarily be among the most popular subjects listed here.
Which subjects did you or do you enjoy most at school? Why? Is it because you were or are good at them, or for other reasons?

2 Before reading the passages, look at the charts on the next page showing how education is organised in Britain and read the notes underneath. Compare the system with the system in your country before going on.

Age	Public Sector (State education)	Private Sector (Independent schools)
3– 5 5–11 11–18	Primary school Comprehensive school Grammar school Secondary-modern school	Playschool, kindergarten Preparatory school Public school Other authorised independent schools
18+	University, College of Further Education, Technical college, Polytechnic	

Notes: Education is compulsory from 5 to 16. About 25%–30% stay on at school beyond this age and about 15% are in full-time education at the age of 20; 10% go to university. About 80% of children in the public sector go to **comprehensive schools**. A few **Local Education Authorities** still retain separation of students into **grammar school** and **secondary-modern school** pupils according to their level.

Preparatory schools are supposed to 'prepare' children for education at a public school.

Public schools were originally founded by public benefactors to educate poor children. In the 19th century, most of them were transformed into **foundations** which are privately run. They are non-profit making, but parents pay **fees** for their children's education.

Colleges of education or **teacher-training colleges** train teachers.

Technical colleges and **polytechnics** offer courses in practical and scientific subjects. Polytechnics award degrees.

University and Polytechnic degree courses last three or four years; the degrees are **BA (Bachelor of Arts)** or **BSc (Bachelor of Science)**. **Postgraduate courses** exist for the degrees of MA (Master of Arts), MSc (Master of Science) and PhD (Doctor of Philosophy).

The three passages that follow refer to one person's education in England. Make sure that you understand the meaning of all the words and phrases in different type. Answer the questions in each case, but at all times compare this account with your own experience.

Primary school

When I first went to school at the age of three, **kindergartens** were not **playschools**. I played in the **playground**, but before I got to primary school I had learned to read and write. At the primary school, there were 42 children in the class; nowadays, the average is 25. We had regular **tests**, with **marks**, and **discipline** was strict. The teacher had a **cane**, which he used if anyone talked or did not **pay attention**. We did not wear **uniforms**, like the children at **preparatory schools**, except for a **cap**, which had the school **badge** on it. The school's main aim was to prepare children for the **11-plus exam**. In the days before comprehensive schools were introduced, all the children in the country took this, and according to the results, were sent to different types of **secondary school**. I went to what was called a direct-grant school; this was a **public school** that accepted over 80% of its intake from state primary schools; the **Local Educational Authority** paid the **fees**, instead of the parents.

a Did you go to a kindergarten or playschool? What did you do there?

b How many children were there in your class at primary school?

c Did you have a lot of tests and exams? Were you given marks regularly for your work?

d Did you wear a uniform?

e Was there corporal punishment of any kind? (see example here)

f Do you think the system at that time was a fair one? Do you think children should be separated at the age of 11 according to an estimate of their ability based on one examination?

g The primary school was co-educational, with boys and girls, but not in the same classes! The direct-grant school only accepted boys. Do you see any advantages of this, or any disadvantage?

Public School

Life at public school was quite different. We had uniforms, and if we did not wear our caps, we were put in **detention** or given **extra work** or some other form of **punishment**. Instead of hours of **arithmetic** and reading and writing, we had **45-minute periods** of various subjects. We went to school six days a week, and there were **compulsory games** on Wednesdays and Saturdays, always the same two games, rugby and cricket. We had an hour's **homework** every night, and sometimes it took longer because we had to learn speeches from Shakespeare **by heart**. But the hours were short. I cycled the five kilometres to school and was usually home by 4.15. In one respect, this school was like a primary school in those days; it was very competitive, though at public school those who got the best marks got **prizes**. All of us were expected to **specialise** at an early age in order to concentrate on the subjects that we would need for **university entrance**. As a result I can count almost as fast as a pocket calculator – I learnt that at primary school – but I know nothing of **algebra** or **geometry** or **physics** or **chemistry**.

When I was about 17, I began to like the school. It had beautiful **grounds** and magnificent **playing fields**, and suddenly the **head** and the **teachers** began to treat us like grown-up people. We had to arrive on time so as not to be marked **absent** in the **attendance register**, but otherwise we were free to pursue our **studies** more or less as we liked. There were no more compulsory games, but plenty of opportunities to take part in other sports we preferred. The only thing we were expected to do in return was to win a **scholarship** to a university so that the school could put our names on a big '**honours board**' in gold letters!

a Did you/do you go to school six days a week? Were/are games compulsory?

b How was/is the curriculum organised? How many periods did/do you have of different subjects?

c Is it common for children to have to learn things by heart in your country? What sorts of things?

d Is there a lot of specialisation in secondary schools? Do you think this is a good thing?

e Why do you think there is a difference in meaning between a **playground** and **playing fields**? What are **grounds** in this context?

f What do you think an 'honours board' was, and why was it important to the school? Why do you think they used 'gold letters'?

g What sort of sports facilities do you think a school should have? Should games be compulsory? If so, what choice of games should be offered to students?

University

Students from other countries that I met at university often took a long time to get used to the system. The university terms lasted only six months and you were free to do what you liked in the **vacations**. Attendance at **lectures** was optional, and the only compulsory **assignment** was to write an **essay** once a week and present it to your **tutor**. The idea was that you were not supposed to be there to obtain an **academic qualification**, but to extend your knowledge of your subject in your own way. It was all there in the **libraries** and **laboratories** and **lecture halls** if you looked for it. A poor American student who had attended all the tutor's lectures once reproduced them almost word for word in his essay, and the tutor said: 'I know what I think. What do you think?' The life of an **undergraduate** was relaxing and enjoyable, but you had to work things out for yourself.

Note: In British universities, there is normally only one **Professor** for a given subject; other university teachers are called **lecturers**. They are also **tutors** when they give individual students classes in small numbers.

a Is this system similar to that of university in your country? If not, what are the differences?

b Why do you think people go to university? Do you think they go for the right reasons?

c What did the American student's tutor expect him to do? How do you suppose this differed from the system he was used to?

Revision

Complete the sentences, using the correct word or phrase from those you have seen above. To help you, the first letter of each word is given.

1 He wants to be a doctor so he is doing three science s_____s at GCSE, b_____, c_____, and p_____.
2 When he has got his d_____ at university, he wants to do a postgraduate c_____ in Germany.
3 I'll give you back your e_____ papers when I've made a note of the m_____s you obtained. It was a difficult t_____, so you did quite well.
4 The little children at the k_____ were playing games in the p_____.
5 He went to a school where the children wore blue and yellow u_____, and the boys had gold b_____s on their c_____.
6 If you don't pay a_____ to what I'm saying, I'll put you in d_____ and you'll have to do some e_____ work.
7 Where were in first p_____ this morning? I've marked you as a_____ in the r_____.
8 I enjoyed his l_____ at the Shakespeare Conference in Stratford.
Yes, he's one of the best l_____s at the university. I expect he'll become the p_____ one day.
9 He wanted his son to study at university but he couldn't afford to pay the f_____s so he was delighted when the boy won a s_____, which covered the cost.
10 Terminology is different at university from what we said at school. At school we said 'holidays', but here they say 'v_____s'; the t_____ here is like the form teacher at school; there they told us to write compositions, here they ask us to write e_____s; and there they talked about homework, but here it's an a_____.

Part B – Verbs

SECTION ONE

1 allow, let, permit

	1	2	6	7	24	29
	−O	O	G	OI	ONC	RI
allow		×	×	×	×	
let				×		×
permit	×	×	×	×	×	

allow
2 *We don't **allow** that sort of behaviour here.*
6 *We don't **allow** smoking in the theatre.*
7 *I'm sorry but we can't **allow** you to take that book out of the library.*
24 *They don't **allow** dogs in the hotel.*

In all these examples, **permit** could be used instead of **allow**, but would always be more formal. In formal contexts, the passive construction is common (see **permit**).
Allow with the gerund (6) refers to general prohibition; where there is a personal object the infinitive construction is used (7).
Noun: **allowance**, money you let someone have regularly.

let (let, let)
7 *She didn't **let** the children go out alone.*
29 **Let** *yourself go!*

Note the form of the infinitive after **let** (without 'to').
Let has no passive form, so example 7 in the passive would become 'The children were not **allowed** (**permitted**) to go out alone'.
Let us (**Let's**) is a more positive form of suggestion than 'Shall we?'. 'Let's have a party' encourages other people, where 'Shall we have a party?' is asking for advice or support. Note that the tag question in this case would be: '**Let's** have a party, shall we?'
Problem: **Let** me come in! (**NOT** leave)
But note: Leave (**Let**) me alone (Don't bother me!). Here both verbs are acceptable.

permit (permitted, permitted)
1 *Play will begin at 2 o'clock weather* **permitting**.
2 *Ball games are not* **permitted** *in the park.*

See **allow**, where **permit** could be substituted in formal contexts in **6, 7** and **24**.
Nouns: **permit**, official document, **permission**, allowing you to do something, (uncountable). **Permit** (noun) is pronounced with stress on the first syllable, the verb and **permission** with the stress on the second.

Complete the sentences, using the correct verb in the appropriate form. Use **allow** rather than **permit** wherever you can.

1 I'm not going to _____ you come into the house with those dirty shoes.
2 I'm not going to _____ you to come into the house with those dirty shoes.
3 Relax! Take it easy! _____ yourself go!
4 _____'s go out and have a good time! Your mother will _____ you to come with us, won't she?
5 Weather _____, we can play this afternoon.
6 We don't _____ dogs in the park unless they are on a lead; we don't _____ camping on the grass, either, so we can't _____ you put up a tent there.
   Aren't we _____ to do anything here, then?

2 arrive, get to, reach

	1	2	3	16	24
	−O	O	PO	NC	ONC
arrive (at, in 2)	×	×			
get to				×	×
reach		×	×		

arrive
1 *They* **arrive** *this morning.*
2 *What time does the train* **arrive at** *the station/in London?*
   They've taken a long time to **arrive at** *a decision.*

The choice of **at** or **in** for places with **arrive** (2) is determined by the size of the place from the speaker's point of view. **In** is normally used for large places (countries, cities). But note that there is no preposition in 'arrive home'.
Noun: **arrival**.
Problem: They **arrived at** the station/**in** London/home. (**NOT** arrived to)

get to
16 *When I* **got to** *the station, the train had left.*
   The news didn't **get to** *me until this afternoon.*
24 *He's very ill. We must* **get** *him* **to** *hospital (***get** *him home).*

Get to implies more difficulty than the others (e.g. in the journey to the station or in the speed of the news **reaching** me) (16).

reach
2 *What time does the train* **reach** *the station/London?*
   Can you **reach** *that book on the top shelf?*
   They've finally **reached** *a decision.*

3 *The news* **reached** *me just as I was going out.*
   Can we **reach** *(contact) him by phone?*

Note the direct object, without preposition, in **2**.
Reach can mean 'be able to touch, get down' (**2**), and so there are the prepositional phrases 'within **reach**' and 'out of **reach**' (that can or cannot be **reached**).
Reach, unlike the other verbs, can take a personal object (**3**).
Noun: **reach**, the distance you can **reach** or the length of your arm ('you have a longer **reach** than I have').

Complete the sentences, using the correct verb in the appropriate form. Pay attention to the structure and the use of prepositions or lack of them, as well as to the meaning.

1 What time did your train _____?
   What time did your train _____ the station?
   What time did your train _____ to the station?
2 The train won't _____ London for half an hour.
   The train won't _____ to London for half an hour.
   The train won't _____ in London for half an hour.
3 What decision did they eventually _____?
   What decision did they eventually _____ at?
4 When you _____ the age of 50, you'll look at things differently.
5 I'm trying to get in touch with Mr Smith. Is there any way of _____ him?
6 Don't worry. We'll _____ you home all right.

3 beat, earn, gain, win

	1	2	3	associations
	−O	O	PO	
beat		×	×	people, record
earn	×	×		money, reward, respect, your living
gain	×	×		advantage, experience, ground, speed, time
win	×	×		game, race, prize, war, bet

beat (beat, beaten)
2 *Liverpool* **beat** *Manchester United (in the final).*
   We've **beaten** *the record.*
3 *I* **beat** *Frank (at chess yesterday).*

As in the cases of the other verbs below, the associations are important. Note that **beat** is the only one that has a personal object, and that it must have an object at all times.
Problem: I **beat** her 6–1. (**NOT** won)

earn

1 *All her children are* **earning** *(money) now.*
2 *How much (money) do you* **earn**?
  His hard work **earned** *our respect.*

Earn suggests 'deserve'; you can **earn** a reward, even if you do not obtain it, but if you **gain** your reward, it is given to you.
Problem: I've **earned** my living since I was 16. (**NOT** gained/won)

gain

1 *My watch has* **gained** *(time).*
2 *I hope to* **gain** *useful experience in my new job.*

Gain suggests 'progress, increase, obtain an advantage', but is not normally used in association with money.
Noun: **gain**, advantage.

win (won, won)

1 *Hurray! We've* **won**.
2 *They* **won** *the game very easily.*

The associations are important; if you **win** money (a prize, a bet) you have not necessarily worked for it, in comparison with **earn**. **Win** has no personal object, like **beat**.
Noun: **win**, victory.

Complete the sentences, using the correct verb in the appropriate tense. Consider the meaning and the phrases commonly used.

1 He _____ £15,000 last year before tax.
2 Our horse has _____ the race! How much have we _____ ?
3 Gold Star was leading until the last 100m in the Grand National but Eagle was _____ ground all the time, and eventually _____ him.
4 She _____ a prize because she _____ the school record in the high jump. She certainly _____ it because she had trained very hard.
5 I don't _____ much money in this job, but I am _____ a lot of useful experience.
6 My watch is fast. It has _____ 10 minutes since yesterday.
7 The general _____ time by avoiding a battle and this eventually helped him to _____ the war.
8 You should go out and _____ your living instead of filling in that coupon, hoping to _____ the football pools.

4 become, develop, grow, grow up

	1	2	15	16	24
	−O	O	AC	NC	ONC
become			×	×	
develop	×	×			
grow	×	×	×	×	×
grow up	×				

become (became, become)
15 *It's* **becoming** *cloudy.*
16 *When did he* **become** *king?*

Become can imply a change of state (**16**) as well as a transition; **grow** could be used in **15** but not in **16**.
Grow is preferred for growth – 'He's **growing** tall'.

develop
1 *The trouble* **developed** *after you had left.*
2 *He needs money to* **develop** *his business.*

Develop means 'show signs of appearing, changing' (**1**) or 'cause to grow, increase' (**2**).
Noun: **development.**

grow (grew, grown)
1 *Nothing* **grows** *in this desert.*
2 *We* **grow** *vegetables in the garden.*
15 *When you* **grow** *old, you'll understand how I feel.*
16 *Oh, you've* **grown** *a beard!*
24 *I've decided to* **grow** *my hair long.*

See **become** (**15**), and note that 'get' could be used there and in example **15** here.
Grow can mean 'develop naturally' (**1**), 'cultivate' (**2**), or 'allow to develop' (**16**), (**24**).
Noun: **growth**, natural development.
Problem: The grass is **growing** tall. (**NOT** growing up)

grow up (grew up, grown up)
1 *What do you want to be when you* **grow up**?

Grow up means 'become adult', and only applies to children, not to animals or plants.
We can also say that 'customs have **grown up**' (developed slowly).
Noun: **grown-up**, child's word for 'adult'.

Complete the sentences, using the correct verb in the appropriate form. Consider the context and meaning as well as the structure.

1 He _____ a beard while he was in hospital.

2 You will have to _____ a more serious attitude toward your work.
3 Since he _____ a member of the Artists' Circle, he's _____ some odd habits.
   For instance, he's _____ his hair long, but he won't _____ an artist by doing that.
4 Your son Andrew has _____ quite tall since I saw him last.
   Yes, he wants to be a policeman when he _____.
5 He's trying to_____ the farm by _____ rice as well as vegetables.
6 When the problem first _____ in the factory, we did not think it was important.
   Now it has _____ so fast that it is getting out of control. (*use two verbs*)

5 borrow, lend

	1	2	3	4
	−O	O	PO	2O
borrow (from 3,4)	×	×	×	×
lend (to 4)		×		×

borrow
1 *I don't approve of* **borrowing**.
2 *May I* **borrow** *your pen?*
3 *He's always* **borrowing** *from his friends.*
4 *I* **borrowed** *this book* *from my uncle.*

The fundamental difference between **borrow** and **lend** is expressed in **4** and **lend** (**4**); you **borrow** things **from** the owner, but the owner **lends** you things/**lends** things **to** you.
Problem: He **borrowed** that pencil **from** me. (**NOT** He borrowed me that pencil.)

lend (lent, lent)
2 *Banks* **lend** *money.*
4 *My uncle* **lent** *me this book/***lent** *this book* *to me.*

See **borrow**.
Noun: **loan,** what is **lent,** usually money.
Problem: **Pay** attention! (**NOT** lend)

Complete the sentences, using the correct verb in the appropriate form. Pay attention to the structure as well as the meaning.

1 I've left my pen at home. Can you _____ me one?
   You can _____ this one, but let me have it back at the end of the lesson.
2 Banks make a profit by _____ money, but they also have to _____ it from time to time.
3 The bank would not _____ him any money, but he managed to _____ what he needed from friends.
4 I don't trust him. He's always _____ from friends and forgetting to pay them back. I wouldn't _____ any money to him if I were you.

5 You can _____ books from the library but they won't _____ you a book
   unless you are a member. They don't _____ books to non-members.

6 bring, carry, fetch, take

	2	4	16	24
	O	2O	NC	ONC
bring	×	×		
carry	×			
fetch	×	×		
take	×	×	×	×

bring (brought, brought)
2 **Bring** *your friends (to the party).*
4 **Bring** *me your homework when you come tomorrow.* (or
   Bring *your homework to me.*)

Bring always means 'towards the speaker'; '**Bring** it here.' Compare to **take**.
Problems:
I've **brought** some friends to tea. (**NOT** taken)
I'll **take** you to the station. (**NOT** bring)

carry (carried, carried)
2 *I'll help you to* **carry** *the cases.*
   The cigarette packet **carries** *(has) a health warning.*
   This aircraft can **carry** *over 500 passengers.*

Carry means **bring/take** people or things from one place to another, but it involves 'bearing the weight of something', except with the special usage of the second example.
Noun: **carriage**, section of a train **carrying** passengers, cost of moving goods from one place to another.
Problems:
Can I **take** you anywhere? (Can I give you a lift?) (**NOT** 'carry' unless you take the person in your arms, or on your shoulders – 'I'll **carry** the baby'.)
Have you **got** your keys with you? (**NOT** Are you carrying your keys?)
She was **wearing** a dress (a necklace, earrings, glasses). (**NOT** 'carrying' for clothing, accessories, etc., but 'She was **carrying** a heavy shopping bag'.)

fetch
2 *Would you like me to* **fetch** *your slippers?*
4 **Fetch** *me a handkerchief from the bedroom, will you?*

Fetch means 'go and get something and bring it back'.

take (took, taken)
2 *I'm going to* **take** *the children to school.*
  You must **take** *the medicine after meals.*
  Keep still, and I'll **take** *your photograph.*
5 *I've* **taken** *her her breakfast (in bed). (I've* **taken** *her breakfast to her.)*
16/24 *How long does it* **take** *(you) to get to work?*
  It **takes** *(me) half an hour.*

The usual meaning of **take** is 'away from the speaker' – '**Take** it over there'. Compare **bring**, and problems with **bring**. But it is also used with a number of expressions with different meanings. Note the following: 'It has **taken** (him) a long time' (**16**), (**24**); '**take** a bus' (catch), '**take** a chance', '**take** a class' (teach, not 'give'), '**take** medicine', '**take** a photograph' (not 'make'), '**take** a seat' (occupy), '**take** a subject' (study).
Problems:
Take me with you. (**NOT** bring/carry)
He **got** very good marks. (**NOT** took)

Complete the sentences, using the correct verb in the appropriate form. Consider the meaning and the structure, and note the examples of phrases given.

1 Mother must have _____ your slippers upstairs, Grandfather. Would you like me to _____ them for you?
2 Happy birthday! I've _____ you a present.
3 The aircraft, which _____ 500 passengers, only _____ five hours to cross the Atlantic.
4 I've left some papers in my office. Wait here while I _____ them.
5 Waiter, this soup is cold. _____ it away and _____ me some fruit juice instead.
6 Is this seat _____? I feel so tired after _____ these parcels all the way to the bus-stop.
7 I _____ a photograph of her on holiday and I've _____ it with me to show her.
8 I must _____ these letters to the post office.
  The postman was _____ a heavy bag of letters.
9 Could you _____ this prescription to the chemist's and _____ me back the medicine. I have to _____ it every night.
10 It doesn't _____ him very long to get to the office.

7 charge, cost, pay

	1	2	3	4	5	7
	−O	O	PO	2O	I	OI
charge (to 2; for 3,4)		×	×	×		
cost		×		×		×
pay (for 3,4)	×	×	×	×	×	×

charge (charged, charged)
2 **Charge** *it* **to** *my account.*
3 *They* **charged** *me* **for** *the room.*
4 *They* **charged** *me £50* **for** *the room.*

Charge means 'record something as owing' (**2**), and 'ask to be paid' (**3**), (**4**). The relationship between the three verbs is as follows:
The shop/hotel **charges** the customer money **for** goods or services.
The goods or services **cost** the customer money.
The customer **pays** the shop/hotel money **for** the goods or services.
Noun: **charge**, price asked or paid – note 'to be **in charge** of' (be responsible **for**), '**take charge of**' (become responsible **for**).

cost (cost, cost)
2 *It* **cost** *too much money.*
4 *The room* **cost** *me £50.*
7 *It* **cost** *me an effort to win the race.* (only with double object)

Cost usually means 'have as a price' (**2**), (**4**).
Compare the examples given under **charge** with **charge** and **pay**.
Noun: **cost**, what something **costs**, – note 'The **cost** of living'. But we normally speak of 'the price' of an object.

pay (paid, paid)
1 *Crime does not* **pay** *(is not worth while).*
2 *Have you* **paid** *the bill?*
3 *Have you* **paid** *her (for her work)?*
4 *I* **paid** *them £50* **for** *the room.*
5 *Did you* **pay** *to come in?*
7 *I* **paid** *them (a lot of money) to do the job.*

Pay means to 'give money for goods, work, etc.'. Compare the examples given under **charge** with **charge** and **cost**. Note the use of 'for' when referring to goods and services.
Pay exists with a number of common phrases: '**pay** a call on', '**pay** a compliment to', '**pay** attention to', '**pay** a visit to'.
We **pay** money into an account or a bank.
Nouns: **pay**, what you regularly earn; **payment**, an amount of money paid, the act of paying.
Problem: He **paid** me **for** the book. (**NOT** paid me the book)

Complete the sentences, using the correct verb in the appropriate tense. Consider the meaning and the structure.

1 How much did they _____ you for the room?
   £50. I said it was too expensive and refused to _____ the bill.
2 How much did the room _____ you?
   Only £40. They wanted to _____ me £50 for it, but I got a reduction.
3 How much did you have to _____ for the room?
   £50. It _____ me more than I expected.
4 It doesn't _____ to argue with them, though. If they take you to court, it will only _____ you more money in the end.

5 I went to _____ some money into the bank, and found my account was overdrawn. The manager asked me to _____ more attention to it in the future.
6 It _____ him a great deal to _____ a compliment to a person he disliked so much.

8 climb, drive, get in(to), get on (to), mount, ride

	1	2	17	23	25
	−O	O	VC	OAC	OVC
climb	×	×			
drive	×	×	×	×	×
get in(to)	×	×			
get on (to)	×	×			
mount	×	×			
ride	×	×	×		×

climb
1 *The road* **climbed** *towards the top of the mountain.*
2 *They have* **climbed** *Mount Everest.*

Climb means 'go up', but implies steepness, difficulty; 'I'm going upstairs', but 'I'm getting too old to **climb** all those stairs'.
Nouns: **climb**, what is climbed; **climber**, of mountains.
Problem: I liked **climbing** trees when I was young. (**NOT** mounting)

drive (drove, driven)
1 *He* **drives** *too fast.*
2 *Can you* **drive** *a car?*
17 **Drive** *to the station.*
23 *That noise is* **driving** *me mad.*
25 **Drive** *me to the airport, please.*

Drive means to 'guide a vehicle', or 'take someone in a vehicle' (25). Compare to **ride** (below), and note that we say 'steer a ship', 'pilot an aircraft', (not **drive**).
Nouns: **drive**, a journey in a vehicle or a private road leading to a house; **driver**, person driving.
Problems:
He **drives** very well. (**NOT** conducts)
A bus conductor sells tickets; a bus **driver** drives the bus. 'A conductor' is the person in charge of an orchestra.
You're **driving** me mad. (**NOT** sending/making)

get in (into) (got in(to), got in(to))
1 **Get in!** *We're in a hurry.*
2 **Get into** *the car! We're in a hurry.*

We **get into** covered vehicles, like cars, but if the action involves climbing steps (some buses and trains, aircraft), we usually say **get on/get on to**. Usage is not clear at present because of the changing design of buses, etc.
Problem: **Get in!** (**NOT** Enter)

get on (on to) (got on (to), got on (to))
1 **Get on!** *You can sit behind me.*
2 **Get on to** *the scooter! You can sit behind me.*

See **get in,** but note that we always **get on to** a bicycle, motor cycle.

mount
1 *They were given the order to* **mount.**
2 *They* **mounted** *their horses.*

Mount is still the correct word for horses, but it is too formal in most contexts for bicycles or motor cycles.
Noun: **mount,** used of horses, but now formal or technical.

ride (rode, ridden)
1 *He* **rides** *very well.*
2 *Can you* **ride** *a bicycle.*
17 **Ride** *to the farm, and get some help.*
25 **Ride** *the donkey to the end of the beach.*

We use **ride,** not **drive,** when we have one leg on either side of the vehicle (motor cycle, bicycle) or for a horse, donkey, etc.
Nouns: **ride,** journey on horse, bicycle, etc.; **rider,** person riding.

Complete the sentences, using the correct verb in the appropriate form. Consider the meaning and the structure. Do not use the same verb twice in the same sentence.

1 He _____ his car and _____ away.
  He _____ his horse and _____ away.
  He _____ his motor cycle and _____ away.
2 These stairs _____ me mad. I find it hard to _____ them, now that I'm getting older.
3 The cyclists have _____ two hundred miles today, and had to _____ a steep hill towards the winning post. I was in a car _____ behind the main group.
4 The Queen, _____ on a white horse, _____ down the line of soldiers, inspecting them. Afterwards, she was _____ up the Mall. Some people had _____ lampposts to get a better view.
5 _____ and I'll _____ you to the station. It's not far, and it's on my way.

9 close, guard, keep, lock, shut

	1	2	6	11	15	17	23	30
	−O	O	G	R	AC	VC	OAC	RAC
close	×	×						
guard		×						
keep	×	×	×	×	×	×	×	×
lock	×	×						
shut	×	×		×				

close (closed, closed)
1 *The shops in this town* **close** *on Wednesday afternoons.*
2 **Close** *the door when you go out, please.*
   The chairman **closed** *the proceedings with a short speech of thanks to those who had been present.*

Close and **shut** are very similar, but **close** is more formal in most contexts. It has the additional meaning of 'bring to an end' (2, second example). We normally use '**close** down' for closing a shop, etc. permanently, and also for the end of broadcasting for the night.

guard
2 *The sentries are* **guarding** *the President's palace.*

Guard is nowadays used only to mean 'protect people or property' or 'prevent from escaping' ('**Guard** the prisoner').
Nouns: **guard,** person in charge of a train, soldier in a regiment originally formed to protect the king or queen, protective covering – **fireguard** in front of a fire, **mudguard** on bicycle; **guardian,** person responsible for orphaned child.
Problem: When you've done the washing-up, **put** the plates **away.** (**NOT** guard them/ keep them)

keep (kept, kept)
1 *I don't think this bread will* **keep** *till the weekend.*
2 *I'm afraid I didn't* **keep** *my promise.*
   Can you **keep** *a secret?*
   They **keep** *chickens.*
6 **Keep** *talking. What you say is interesting.*
11 *He doesn't earn enough to* **keep** *himself and his family.*
15 *I'm wearing a heavy coat to* **keep** *warm.*
17 **Keep** *to the right as you go along the corridor.*
23 *That will* **keep** *them busy for a time.*
30 *I like to do some work, although I've retired, to* **keep** *myself busy.*

Keep means 'remain in its present state' (**1**), 'continue' (**6**), (**15**), (**17**), 'maintain' (**23**), (**30**). It is found with a number of expressions, meaning 'maintain', 'retain', 'have and look after' (**2**), (**11**).

Noun: **keeper**, person who looks after animals in a zoo, etc., and also in combinations – **shopkeeper**, **housekeeper**, etc.
Problem: **Keep** this for me until I come back. (**NOT** 'guard' unless the person spoken to is a guard.)

lock
1 *I can't get this door to* **lock** *properly.*
2 **Lock** *the door when you go out.*

To **lock** is to **close/shut** with a key, bolt, etc. So we can say: 'He **shut** the door but forgot to **lock** it.' **Lock up** is to **shut up** completely: 'They've **locked up** the house for the holidays because they won't be back for a fortnight' (**locked** all the windows, doors, etc., **locked** valuable things in a safe place).
Nouns: **lock**; **locker**, where clothes are kept at school, in a club, etc.

shut (shut, shut)
1 *Why doesn't this door* **shut**?
2 *I've* **shut** *the gate.*
11 *Don't* **shut** *yourself (up) in your room when people come to the house.*

Similar to **close**, and more common. Note the expression '**Shut up!**' (Be quiet!). **Shut (up)** also has the meaning of 'enclose, imprison' (**11**).
Noun: **shutter**, wood or metal cover over windows or shops, and also part of a camera that opens when the picture is taken.
Problem: **Keep** your mouth **shut** and don't tell anyone what you have seen. (**NOT** Close your mouth)

Complete the sentences, using the correct verb in the appropriate form. Consider the meaning as well as the structure.

1 He has a housekeeper to _____ house for him and a guard dog to _____ it at night.
2 I'm sorry I failed to _____ my appointment with you last week. I suddenly remembered that when I _____ up the shop, I _____(or_____) the back door, but forgot to _____ it. The money was all _____ up in the safe but I was afraid that a thief might break in.
3 _____ quiet while Susan is reading! _____ up, I say!
4 When she started _____ a diary, she was afraid her brothers might read it so she _____ it up in her desk, and hid the key.
5 The crown jewels are _____ up in a glass case, and _____ by soldiers. You have to _____ in a line as you go round the room. Of course, anyone who tried to steal them would be _____ up.
6 I see you have all _____ (or _____) your books. If you've finished your work, you can write ten sentences using these verbs. That will _____ you busy for a while.

10 discover, find, find out, get to know, meet

	1	2	4	7	9	10	12	13	14	23	25	30	32
	-O	O	2O	OI	OP	2OI	TH	QW	QWI	OAC	OVC	RAC	RVC
discover		×		×			×	(×)	(×)				
find		×	×		×	×	×			×	×	×	×
find out	×	×					×	×	×				
get to know		×											
meet	×	×											

discover

2 *Columbus* discovered *America.*
   Fleming discovered *penicillin.*
7 *We knew nothing about her when she came here, but we've* discovered *her to be the perfect secretary.*
12 *I've* discovered *that your grandfather knew my father.*

Discover is used for finding things that were not previously known about, but existed. So we discover a cure for an illness, but 'invent' a machine, something that originates in the inventor's mind.
Discover and find out can often be used in the same sentence (example 12 here, and find out (13) and (14) below); discover is more formal and find out implies looking for the fact or answer, not obtaining it by chance.
Nouns: discovery, what is discovered; discoverer, the person who discovers, normally used only of famous people like Columbus, Fleming, etc.
Problem: Columbus discovered America. (NOT found)

find (found, found)

2 *I've* found *my umbrella. I thought I had lost it.*
4 *She* found *the tramp some old clothes (*found *some old clothes for the tramp).*
9 *They* found *the children playing in the garden.*
10 *You're wet. I'll* find *you something to put on.*
12 *We* found *that the new washing powder didn't work very well.*
23 *I* found *her very helpful.*
25 *We* found *him in bed with a bad cold.*
30 *I* find *myself unable to give him a satisfactory answer.*
32 *When he woke up, he* found *himself in hospital.*

Find usually relates to people or things lost or hidden (2), but can also mean 'look for, to provide someone with' (4), (10), 'discover by experience' (12), (23), (30), or 'discover, by chance' (9), (25), (32). In those relating to experience, the sentences could be rewritten with 'prove' – 'She proved very helpful' (compare to example 23).

find out (found out, found out)

1 *I'm not going to tell you the answer.* Find out *(for) yourself.*
2 *I've* found out *her secret. She's engaged to John.*

13 *Have you* **found out** *where he lives?*
14 *We must* **find out** *how to do it.*

Find out means '**discover** or learn something, usually hidden' and involves asking questions, making an effort. See **discover**, above.

get to know (got to know, got to know)
2 *It's not easy to* **get to know** *people in this village.*

Getting to know a person or country is an intermediate stage between **meeting** the person or visiting the country for the first time and **knowing** them.
Problem: I want to go to England to **get to know** the people and the country. (**NOT** know)

meet (met, met)
1 *I think we should* **meet** *to discuss it tomorrow.*
2 *I* **met** *her at a party.*

Meet means 'come together' (with a person) by arrangement, if you already know them (**1**), or by chance, if you do not (**2**). Note 'I've never **met** her. You must introduce me to her.'
Noun: **meeting**, when people come together (not usually 'reunion', which is a **meeting** of old friends, comrades who **meet** again after a period of time).
Problems:
Have you ever **met** my husband? (**NOT** found/encountered)
I **met** Mrs Smith in the street just now. (**NOT** found/encountered)

Complete the sentences, using the correct verb in the appropriate form. Consider the meaning as well as the structure.

1 I'm going to _____ my brother at the airport. Would you like to come with me?
   Yes, I've never _____ him. I'd like to come.
   You may _____ him a little shy when you first _____ him, but once you _____ him he's a charming person.
2 Doctors have been trying to _____ (*or* _____) what causes the disease for a long time but they're _____ it very difficult.
3 I've just _____ (*or* _____) that we're related. Apparently one of my cousins _____ a cousin of yours on holiday last year. They _____ each other, and they've just got married.
   That's funny. I _____ it very strange that I haven't heard about it. What are their names?
4 I was looking for Simon all morning, and couldn't _____ him. In the end I _____ him hiding in the coal cellar.
5 We'll _____ outside the restaurant at 8.30. Don't worry about missing the last bus. We can easily _____ you a bed for the night.
6 When I woke up after the accident, I _____ myself in hospital. The worst of it was that I _____ that I couldn't move my legs. It took me a minute or two to _____ (*or* _____) where the bell was and ring for the nurse.

11 dress, put on, wear

	1 −O	2 O	15 AC	23 OAC
dress	×	×	×	×
put on		×		
wear	×	×	×	×

dress
1 *I'll be ready in a minute. I'm* **dressing.** (**getting dressed** is less formal, and more common.)
2 *Help me to* **dress** *the children, will you?*
15 *She* **dresses** *very well.*
23 *They* **dressed** *the children in cowboy suits.*

Dress means 'put on clothes (1), or 'put them **on** other people' (2), (23), but note 'get **dressed**' (1). In 15 it means 'choose (appropriate) clothes to **wear**'. **Be dressed in . . .** is an informal alternative for **wear** (see **wear**).
Nouns: **dress,** clothing in general, garment worn only by women; **dressmaker,** person who makes **dresses** for women.
Problems:
It's time to **get dressed.** (**NOT** dress yourself)
Lay (Set) the table. (**NOT** Dress)

put on (put on, put on)
2 *She* **put on** *her shoes (put her shoes* **on***) and went out.*
   I **put** *my clothes* **on.** (I **got dressed** is more common.)

Put on means 'place on the body', and can be used for e.g. jewellery, a watch, apart from clothes. It has other meanings – 'increase' (**put on** weight), 'turn on' (**put on** the light).
Problem: **Put** your hat **on!** (**NOT** 'wear' – When you have **put** it **on,** you will be **wearing** it.)

wear (wore, worn)
1 *The carpet has* **worn,** *and must be repaired.*
2 *You're* **wearing** *a new dress, aren't you? (You've got a new dress on, haven't you?* which is less formal.)
15 *She was* **wearing** *blue (She was* **dressed in** *blue).*
23 *The old soldier* **wore** *medals on his uniform.*

Wear means 'be **dressed in**' (2), (15), but we could not use the alternative in 23 because medals are not clothes; note '**wear** a watch'. It also means 'be reduced' (1), usually by rubbing against something, or 'last, in spite of this' – 'These shoes have **worn** very well'.
Noun: **wear,** use that reduces or damages material, or the quality of lasting in spite of this.

Problems:
He was **wearing** a watch. (**NOT** 'carrying' if it was attached to his body)
She always **wears** black/She is always **dressed in** black. (**NOT** She always puts on black)

Complete the sentences, using the correct verb in the appropriate form. Pay attention to the structure as well as the meaning and use the alternatives **get dressed** and **be dressed in** where possible.

1 She always takes a long time to _____ (*or* _____) before a party.
2 _____ and come shopping with me. I want to buy a new dress to _____ at the party.
3 The bride is going to _____ white (*or* _____ in white), of course.
4 She _____ the children, and made sure that they _____ their overcoats before they went out. She was afraid that they would catch cold if they were not _____ warm clothes.
5 You'll find these shoes _____ well, sir. _____ them _____ and see if they fit you.
6 She has wonderful taste and _____ beautifully though of course she's lucky to have so many clothes to _____.

12 educate, instruct, learn, study, teach, train

	1	2	4	5	7	12	13	14	22
	–O	O	2O	I	OI	TH	QW	QWI	OQWI
educate		×			×				
instruct (in 4)		×	×						
learn	×	×		×		×	×	×	
study	×	×		×					
teach	×	×	×		×	×			×
train	×	×		×	×				

educate (educated, educated)
2 *It's the school's responsibility to* **educate** *children.*
7 *We must* **educate** *them to play their part in society.*

Educate has to do with training people's minds and characters, but parents 'bring up' their children (care for them, **teach** them how to behave).
Noun: **education**, at school, not 'upbringing' or 'good manners'.
Problems:
You have **brought up** your children very well; they are very polite. (**NOT** 'educated', except academically – 'He is well **educated**; he went to Oxford'.)
He is well **brought up**; he never shouts or is rude. (**NOT** educated)

instruct
2/4 *She* **instructed** *them (***in** *new methods).*

Instruct is a more formal word than **teach** or **train**; it often implies demonstration, where **train** implies physical practice of techniques. Nevertheless, the real difference is that of usage, connected with the nouns.
Nouns: **instruction; instructor,** (skiing, swimming, dancing, flying) – **teacher** could be used for the less technical skills of swimming and dancing.
Problem: I **instructed** him **in** new techniques. (**NOT** I instructed him new techniques)

learn (learned/learnt, learned/learnt)
1   *You'll never* **learn** *if you don't study.*
2   *Have you* **learnt** *a lot at school this year?*
5   *Have you* **learnt** *to drive yet?*
12 *I've* **learned** *that there is no substitute for experience.*
13 *I've* **learned** *what the symptoms of the disease are.*
14 *I've* **learnt** *how to operate the machine.*

Teachers **teach** students subjects or techniques; students **learn** subjects or techniques **from** teachers.
You **study** in order to **learn**; in theory, the more you **study**, the more you **learn**.
Nouns: **learner; learning,** the process or the knowledge eventually acquired.
Problem: I've come here to **learn** English. (**NOT** know)

study (studied, studied)
1   *I've been* **studying** *all morning.*
2   *What subjects do you* **study** *at school?*
5   *He's* **studying** *to be a doctor.*

See **learn.**
Nouns: **student,** person; **study,** work or place.
Problem: He is **studying** at the university. (**NOT** learning)

teach (taught, taught)
1   *I* **teach** *at the local primary school.*
2   *I* **teach** *English.*
4   *We* **taught** *them a great deal.*
7   *You must* **teach** *them to work things out for themselves.*
12 *Experience* **teaches** *(us) that we must treat people as human beings, not like numbers.*
22 *I've* **taught** *them how to answer that sort of question.*

See **instruct. Teach** is a more generally used word.
Nouns: **teaching,** what is taught; **teacher,** person.
Problem: I've **taught** them everything I know. (**NOT** learnt)

train
1   *He* **trains** *for the big race in the evenings.*
2   *He* **trains** *animals (in the circus).*
5   *He's* **training** *to be a doctor.*
7   *They* **train** *horses to jump over fences.*

Train is applied to physical practice (1), (2), (7). In example 5, it suggests practical experience in hospitals rather than reading medical books; see **study**, same example.
Noun: **training**, practice, and results of practice – 'The soldiers' **training** showed on the field of the battle; they fought well because they have been well **trained**.'; trainer, teaching exercises of physical nature to people, animals, but in special contexts, e.g. **teacher trainer**, person who **instructs teachers** in techniques.

Complete the sentences, using the correct verb in the appropriate form. Consider the meaning and the structure and also pay attention to the context. Use each verb only once in the same sentence.

1 You cannot expect to _____ people properly unless you _____ the latest books on the subject and _____ new techniques. If you go on a teacher _____ course, they will _____ you in new methods.
2 It's not enough to _____ children English in the classroom. They have to _____ at home as well.
3 Some parents expect the school to _____ their children manners, as well as to _____ them.
4 He _____ medicine at university and now he's _____ to be a doctor at a hospital in London.
5 She _____ at a school for handicapped children, where the boys and girls _____ to look after themselves.
6 When I started _____ athletes for the Olympic Games, one of the first things I had to do was to _____ them how to relax.
7 You can't expect children to _____ how to do things unless you've _____ them how to do them.
8 Experience has _____ me students _____ best if they are encouraged.

13 expect, hope, look forward to, wait

	1	2	5	6	7	8	12	19
	−O	O	I	G	OI	OG	TH	SO
expect		×	×		×		×	×
hope (for 2)		×	×				×	×
look forward to		×		×		×		
wait (for 2,7)	×	×	×		×			

expect
2 *I'm* **expecting** *a letter from her.*
5 *I* expect *to receive an answer soon.*
7 *She* expects *students to arrive on time.*
12 *I* expect *that you're feeling tired after that long journey.*
19 *Will they be there tomorrow? I* **expect** *so.*

Expect refers to what we think will happen (good or bad) in the future; in example 7, the meaning is close to 'require', and in **12** to 'suppose'.
Noun: **expectation**, waiting believing that something will happen, or the state of **expecting**.

hope (hoped, hoped)
2 *We were* **hoping for** *better news.*
5 *I* **hope** *to see them next week.*
12 *I* **hope** *that they'll be able to come, but I'm not sure.*
19 *Will it be a fine day tomorrow? I* **hope** *so.*

Hope refers to what we want to happen in the future (good), whether we think it will or not. Compare **expect**.
Noun: **hope**.
Problem: We're **hoping for** good weather tomorrow. (**NOT** hoping good weather)

look forward to
2 *We're* **looking forward to** *the party.*
6 *I* **look forward to** *seeing you next Tuesday.*
8 *I* **look forward to** *them (their) visiting us.*

Look forward to means '**expect** to be pleased by . . .', so it combines the idea of **expect** and **hope**. Consequently, it is conventionally used as the ending to a letter: 'I **look forward to** hearing from you,'; you **expect** an answer for reasons of politeness and also **hope for** one, since you want to know what the other person will say. Note that **look forward to** is followed by the gerund, not the infinitive (**6**), (**8**).
Problem: I'm **looking forward to** hearing from you. (**NOT** looking forward to hear/ expecting to hear/waiting to hear)

wait
1 *I'm sorry, but he's busy. Do you mind* **waiting** *here?*
2 *They were* **waiting for** *the bus.*
5 *They've been* **waiting** *to come in for half an hour.*
7 *I was* **waiting for** *them to explain what had happened.*

Wait is an activity, whereas the other verbs reflect states of mind. Note the use of **for** when the verb takes an object.
Nouns: **wait** ('a long **wait**'); **waiter/waitress** – they **wait on** customers, **wait for** orders.
Problem: **Wait for** me! (**NOT** Wait me)

Complete the sentences, using the correct verb in the appropriate tense. Consider the meaning of the sentence to decide which verb is best, but also consider the structure, referring to the chart and examples if necessary.

1 We _____ them to arrive in time for dinner.
2 I _____ seeing you again soon.
3 I'm sorry you are ill, and _____ (that) you'll feel better soon.
4 I've been _____ for the bus for half an hour.
5 We can't get in. We'll have to _____ until they come home.
6 I _____ (that) it won't rain tomorrow. We want to play tennis.
   I _____ (that) you'll be able to. The weather forecast is good.
7 He's very late. I _____ he has missed his train.

He's very late. I _____ nothing has happened to him.

8 We're _____ the party on Saturday. I'm sure we'll enjoy ourselves.

9 Thank you again for your letter. We _____ hearing from you.

10 Will they be all right on their own?

I _____ so. They're old enough to look after themselves.

Will they be all right on their own?

I _____ so. But I can't help worrying about them.

14 intend, mean, plan, try

	1	2	4	5	6	7	12	16	26
	−O	O	2O	I	G	OI	TH	NC	OAS
intend		×	×	×		×	×		×
mean		×	×	×	×	×	×	×	×
plan	×	×		×			×		×
try	×	×		×	×				×

intend

2 *What do you* **intend**? *(What have you got in mind?)*

4 *We didn't* **intend/mean** *them any harm.*

5 *I* **intend/mean** *to settle this matter immediately.*

7 *I* **intended/meant** *it to be a surprise.*

12 *I* **intend** *that they should have a good education.*

26 *I* **intended/meant** *it as a joke.*

Intend and **mean** are similar in meaning, but **mean** has the additional meanings of 'intend to say' and 'indicate'. In examples **4**, **5**, **7** and **26 intend** is more formal and less common in everyday usage.

Noun: **intention.**

Problems:

He's **attempting** a world record jump. (**NOT** intending)

He **tried** to convince me by using all kinds of arguments. (**NOT** 'intended' unless he gave up the idea.)

He **intends** to come with us. (**NOT** pretends)

mean (meant, meant)

2 *What does that word* **mean**?

I **meant** *Thursday morning, not Thursday afternoon.*

6 *If you go via Madrid, it* **means** *waiting at the airport.*

12 *I* **meant** *that you looked tired, not old.*

16 *Those black clouds* **mean** *rain.*

See also examples given above with **intend**.

Noun: **meaning,** what something indicates, what you **mean** to say.

Problem: What does he **mean** by that? (**NOT** want to say)

plan (planned, planned)
1 *You must* **plan** *ahead.*
2 *I'm* **planning** *a visit to Italy.*
5 *I* **plan** *to catch the 12.00 train.*
12 *We've* **planned** *that the concert should start at 8.*
26 *I* **planned** *it as a surprise party.*

Plan implies organising future activity in a logical way, making **plans**, where **intend** simply implies having the idea, having **intentions**.
Nouns: **plan**; **planning**, the action of making **plans**.
Problem: I'm **planning** a visit to Italy. (**NOT** 'intending' – I **intend** to go to Italy.)

try (tried, tried)
1 *I don't think you were* **trying**.
2 **Try** *that hotel, and see if you like it.*
5 *They are* **trying** *to solve the problem.*
6 **Try** *doing it that way. You'll find it easier.*
26 *Why don't you* **try** *it as an experiment.*

Try means 'make an effort' (**1**), (**5**) and 'make an experiment' (**2**), (**6**), (**26**). Note the difference in meaning in using the gerund (**6**) and infinitive (**5**).
Noun: **trial**, act of judging in court, 'be **on trial**', and test, 'motor cycle **trial**', 'trial period' in a job.
Problem: **Try** it. I'm sure you'll like it. (**NOT** prove)

Complete the sentences, using the correct verb in the appropriate form. Consider the meaning and the structure. Use **mean** rather than **intend**, wherever possible.

1 I'm not sure what you _____ in this composition. It's not bad but you must _____ harder. In the first place, you must _____ your compositions in advance.
2 If you're _____ ahead for next summer and you _____ to enjoy yourself, _____ joining our group holidays for young people.
3 We _____ it as a joke. We didn't _____ that anyone should get hurt. (*use two verbs to improve the style.*)
4 Those clouds _____ rain, so if you're _____ a picnic, you may be disappointed.
5 Oh, dear, I've erased the computer's memory of that. That _____ doing it all over again.
6 We don't _____ them any harm, but we _____ that they should learn to respect us. (*use two verbs to improve the style.*)
7 If you feel strong enough, _____ to get up by yourself.
8 I realise now that he was _____ to tell the way to the house, but I didn't understand what he _____.

15 lay, lie, lie

	1	2	15	17	25
	−O	O	AC	VC	OVC
lay		×			×
lie			×	×	
lie (to 2)	×	×			

lay (**laid, laid,** present participle, **laying**)
2 *Bricklayers* **lay** *bricks.*
   How many eggs have the hens **laid** *today?*
   Would you mind **laying** *the table.*
25 **Lay** *it on the table in the kitchen.*

The main thing to remember is that **lay** takes a direct object and the other verbs do not. The general meaning is 'put down': '**lay** the table' means put the cloth, plates, etc., on the table before a meal.

lie (**lay, lain,** present participle, **lying**)
15 *Don't move!* **Lie** *still!*
17 *The village* **lies** *at the foot of the hill.*
    He **lay** *on the floor, too tired to move.*

Lie means 'to be in a place, especially in a flat, resting position'.
Problem: All the errors made by confusing **lay** and **lie** are made because of uncertainty about forms and forgetting the structures, which are never the same (see chart above).

lie (**lied, lied,** present participle, **lying**)
1 *That's not true! He's* **lying!**
2 *You* **lied** *to the court when you gave evidence at the trial.*

This **lie** means 'not tell the truth'. It should never be confused in context with the others, and has different forms, except for the present participle, **lying.**
Nouns: **lie**; **liar**, person who tells **lies.**

Complete the sentences, paying particular attention to the forms when using the verbs in the appropriate tense. Consider the meaning and the structure.

1 I have a headache, I'm going to _____ down.
2 She helped her mother to _____ the table.
3 Our hens _____ a lot of eggs yesterday.
4 Can't you see that he was _____? It was obviously not true.
5 _____ still, or they'll see us.
6 He _____ there for half an hour before someone noticed him.
7 Those paintings have been _____ in the store-room for years.
8 When he had _____ ill for a long time, he slowly began to recover.
9 It's no use _____ the blame on them. It's not their fault.
10 The builder _____ strong foundations to the house.

16 pass, spend, waste

	1	2	4	9
	−O	O	2O	OP
pass (to 1,4)	×	×	×	
spend (on 2)		×		×
waste (on 2)		×		×

pass
1 *The road was so narrow that there was only room for one car to* **pass** *at a time.*
  I'm sorry that you didn't **pass** *(the test).*
  He **passed** *(the ball)* to *me.*
2 *He* **passed** *the time, while he was waiting, doing a crossword puzzle.*
4 **Pass** *me the sugar, will you?* (**Pass** *the sugar* to *me*).

Pass means 'go forward', 'be successful (in a test, exam)', and 'transfer to another person'. It can also mean 'overtake' – 'We **passed** several other cars on the road'.
The difference between **passing** and **spending** time is that we **pass** time doing things to avoid being bored – see **pastime**.
Nouns: **pass**, printed permission, allowing you to **pass**, level showing you have **passed** a test, act of transferring ball to another player in a game; **passage**, narrow way through, piece of writing, course of time, long sea journey; **passenger**; **passport**; **pastime**, something done to **pass** the time in an agreeable way, like crossword puzzles.
Problems:
What has **happened**? (**NOT** passed)
I'm glad you **passed** the examination. (**NOT** approved)
I think this cheese has **gone off** (gone bad). (**NOT** passed)

spend (spent, spent)
2 *We've* **spent** *a lot of money* (**on** *the house*).
  He has **spent** *his whole life in the village.*
9 *He* **spends** *his time gardening.*

We can **spend** money or time **on** *things*. For **spending** time, see **pass**.
Nouns: **expenditure**, what is **spent**; **expense**, cost; **expenses**, costs for a purpose, usually business.
Problems:
What size shoes do you **take**? (**NOT** spend)
He **spends** every weekend at his house in the country. (**NOT** passes)

waste (wasted, wasted)
2 *You shouldn't* **waste** *your money* (**on** *things like that*).
9 *He* **wastes** *his time playing silly games.*

Waste means to **spend** (money or time) badly; the same constructions are used.
Noun: **waste**, wrong use, unwanted matter (chemical **waste**), empty, unused area of land (polar **wastes**).

Complete the sentences, using the correct verb in the appropriate form. Consider the meaning and the structure.

1 He _____ the whole day repairing the toy, but the child broke it immediately, so he decided he had been _____ his time.
2 As time _____, and he grew older, he wondered if he had _____ his life because he had never achieved very much, but he was convinced that on the whole he had _____ it usefully.
3 _____ me the newspaper, will you? I'll do the crossword. At least it will help to _____ the time until our guests arrive.
4 I'd rather _____ my holiday working in the garden than _____ money on trips abroad that I wouldn't enjoy.
5 He's _____ so much time and money on his motor cycle, improving its performance, that he's not happy unless he can _____ every car on the road.

17 play, practise, train

	1	2	4	5	6	7	18
	−O	O	2O	I	G	OI	AS
play (on, for 4)	×	×	×				
practise	×	×			×		×
train	×	×		×		×	

play
1 *Are you coming out to* **play***?*
2 *I'm* **playing** *tennis this afternoon.*
   Can you **play** *the piano?*
   He **played** *the part of Hamlet at school.*
4 **Play** *me your favourite record.*
   Play *me a tune/***Play** *a tune* **for** *me/***Play** *me something* **on** *the piano.*

Play means 'take part in a game' (**1**), (**2**), but also 'know how to use a musical instrument' (**2**), 'perform a piece of music' or 'put it on a record player' (**4**). It also means 'act in a play' (**2**) when associated with the part or character – 'He **played** Hamlet'.
We **play** games (football, tennis, chess, etc.) but we 'do' or 'take part in' sports; there is usually a special verb in these cases, 'swim', 'ski', 'run', etc.
Nouns: **play**, the action of a game (but not the tactical action, which is 'move'), a piece of work written for the theatre; **player** (of games) – 'tennis **player**', though there are some special words, 'footballer', 'golfer', etc.; musicians are defined by their instrument – 'pianist', 'violinist', 'guitarist'; people who act in plays are 'actors'.
Problems:
He can **play** the piano very well. (**NOT** touch)
He can **play** the guitar. (**NOT** play guitar)
That was a brilliant **move**. It deserved to produce a goal. (**NOT** play)
We had a very good **game**. (**NOT** play)

practise (practised, practised)

1 *He is not making much progress with the violin because he hasn't got time to* **practise**.
2 *He's* **practising** *a piece of music for the concert.*
6 **Practise** *playing the melody without the accompaniment.*
18 *He* **practises** *as a lawyer.*

Practise means 'prepare for a game, sport, or musical performance by doing exercises; actors 'rehearse'. It can also mean 'exercise a profession' (**18**).
Noun: **practice**, preparation for game, concert, etc., the regular work of a doctor or lawyer, course of action (compared to 'principle' or 'theory') – note 'in **practice**'.
Problem: Do you **do/go in for** any sports? (**NOT** practise)

train

1 *He's* **training** *for the big race next weekend.*
2 *He* **trains** *horses.*
5 *He's* **training** *to be a doctor.*
7 *He* **trains** *dogs to do tricks.*

Train means 'prepare for a sport' (**1**), 'prepare a person or animal for a sport or performance' (**2**), (**7**), 'prepare oneself for a profession' (**5**). **Train** (**1**) means physical exercise – running, etc., where **practise** (**1**) in sports means trying out tactical moves.
Nouns: **training**, preparation or the time spent on it; **trainer**, usually in charge of physical preparation of players, not technical aspects – 'coach'.

Complete the sentences, using the correct verb in the appropriate form. Consider the meaning and the structure.

1 I don't want to _____ football this afternoon because I'm _____ for the Marathon on Saturday.
2 Why don't you _____ that tune for me that you _____ last week?
   I don't really want to. I've been _____ it all week and I'm not happy about it yet.
3 He's _____ to be a doctor, and if he passes his exams, he will start _____ as a doctor next year.
4 I've been _____ the team to take penalty kicks, and they've been _____ shooting at the goal all afternoon, but I hope we _____ well enough to win the game without deciding it that way.
5 Can you _____ this tune on the piano?
   I can't _____ anything well unless I _____ beforehand.
6 _____ me the piece you composed for the performance when you _____ the part of Othello.

18 prove, test, try, try on, try out, turn out

	1	2	5	6	7	12	15	16	23	26
	–O	O	I	G	OI	TH	AC	NC	OAC	OAS
prove		×	×		×	×	×	×	×	
test	×	×								
try	×	×	×	×						×
try on		×								
try out		×								
turn out	×	×	×			×	×	×		

prove (proved, proved)
2   That **proves** the truth of what I said.
5   His guess **proved** (to be) correct.
7   The evidence **proved** him to have been involved in the robbery.
12   That **proves** that he had nothing to do with it.
15   His guess **proved** correct.
16   The painting **proved** (to be) a fake.
23   The evidence **proved** him guilty.

Prove has two main meanings – 'demonstrate' (2), (7), (8), (12), (23), and '**turn out**', 'be eventually shown to be' (5), (15), (23). Where **turn out** can be substituted for **prove, turn out** is more informal.
Noun: **proof**, demonstration that something is true, printed version to be checked and corrected before printing.
Problem: His evidence **proved** false. (**NOT** resulted)

test
1   No one can hear you. We're just **testing** (making a test).
2   The optician **tested** my eyes.

Test means 'make a test', 'examine by making a test'.
Noun: **test**.

try (tried, tried)
1   I don't think you were **trying**.
2   **Try** that hotel, and see if you like it.
5   They are **trying** to solve the problem.
6   **Try** doing it that way. You'll find it easier.
26   Why don't you **try** it as an experiment?

Try means 'make an effort' (1), (5) and 'make an experiment' (2), (6), (26). Note the difference in meaning between using the infinitive (5) and the gerund (6).
Noun: **trial**, act of judging in court, 'be on **trial**', test in the sense of 'motor-cycle **trial**', '**trial** period' in a job.
Problem: **Try** it! I'm sure you'll like it! (**NOT** prove)

try on (tried on, tried on)
2 *Can I* **try** *this coat* **on**, *please?*

You **try on** clothes to see if you like them or if they are the right size. Compare **try out**.
Problem: Can I **try** *this* **on**? (**NOT** Can I prove it?)

try out (tried out, tried out)
2 *Would you like to* **try out** *this recipe?*

Try out means 'make an experiment with . . . , to see if you like it'. It is used for ideas, methods, cars, etc., but not for clothes (see **try on**).
Problem: I'll **try** it **out**, and let you know if it works. (**NOT** prove)

turn out
1 *I tried out your recipe for cakes.*
    Oh! How did they **turn out**?
2 **Turn out** *the light. (***Turn** *the light* **out**).
5 *The stranger* **turned out** *to be her cousin.*
12 *It* **turned out** *that he had just arrived from Australia.*
15 *I'm glad the weather has* **turned out** *fine.*
16 *The party* **turned out** *(to be) a success.*

Turn out usually means 'happen to be in the end'; see **prove**. It also has other meanings, such as 'put out' (**2**), notably 'send away', 'They **turned** me **out** because I didn't pay the rent'; 'produce', 'The factory **turns out** 100 cars a day'; 'empty of contents', 'I'm **turning out** these cupboards'.
Problem: He **turned out** to be her cousin. (**NOT** resulted)

Complete the sentences, using the correct verb in the appropriate form. Consider the meaning and the structure.

1 _____ it _____, and see if it fits you.
2 I want to _____ your memory. _____ to remember everything you did yesterday morning.
   All right, I'll _____, but will it _____ anything?
   I think so. _____ writing things down if it will help you.
3 If my theory is correct, it will solve your problems. I'm going to _____ it _____, anyway.
4 The evidence _____ him guilty. It _____ that the person he had offered the drugs to was a policeman.
5 It's _____ to be a fine day, after all. That _____ that the people who do the weather forecast don't know their job.
6 We _____ a different hotel for our holiday this year, but it _____ (*or* _____) very expensive.

19 remember, remind

	1	2	3	4	5	6	7	12	13	20
	−O	O	PO	2O	I	G	OI	TH	QW	OTH
remember	×	×	×		×	×		×	×	
remind (of 4)			×	×			×			×

remember
1 *I'm sorry. I don't* **remember** *(what happened).*
2 *I don't* **remember** *his address.*
3 *I* **remember** *her very well.*
5 *I must* **remember** *to ask her about it.*
6 *I* **remember** *spending many happy holidays there.*
12 **Remember** *that the Smiths are coming to dinner.*
13 *I don't* **remember** *where she lives.*

Remember has two main meanings – 'to have the memory of' (**1**), (**2**), (**3**), (**6**), (**13**), and 'not forget' (**5**), (**12**). Note that the use of the gerund means 'have the memory of', and of the infinitive means 'not forget'.
Nouns: **memory**, the part of the brain that **remembers**, what you **remember**; a **remembrance** is an object of sentimental value making you **remember** the past, but we usually say 'souvenir'.

remind
3 *That* **reminds** *me. I have to post a letter.*
4 *It* **reminds** *me* **of** *home.*
  The picture **reminded** *me* **of** *you.*
7 **Remind** *me to post that letter.*
20 *Your saying that* **reminds** *me that I have to buy something.*

Remind means 'make someone **remember**, recall' (**3**), (**4**), (**20**), and 'make someone not forget' (**7**), where it takes the infinitive – see **remember**. **Remind** always has a personal object.
Noun: **reminder**, to prevent someone from forgetting.
Problems:
Remind me to do it. (**NOT** remember)
It **reminds** me of you. (**NOT** remembers)

Complete the sentences, using the correct verb in the appropriate form. Be careful with the structure.

1 That _____ me of the place where I grew up.
2 Do you _____ missing the bus last winter, and having to walk?
  Don't _____ me. I caught a terrible cold, and was in bed for three weeks afterwards.
3 Please _____ to post that letter on your way to work, and _____, too, that there won't be anybody in when you come home. Anne rang up to _____ me that I have to go to the school meeting.
4 That picture _____ me of someone I know. Do you _____ the face?

Yes, but I can't _____ where I have seen it before.
5 Do you _____ that couple we met at Bath last year? Well, that's the husband.
Seeing him again _____ me that we didn't send them a Christmas card.

20 rob, steal

	2	4	
	O	2O	
rob (4 of)	×	×	
steal (4 from)	×	×	

rob (robbed, robbed)
2 *They've* **robbed** *me.*
   They **robbed** *the bank.*
4 *He* **robbed** *me* **of** *my good name.*

People and places are **robbed**; objects are **stolen**. Note the prepositions used after the two verbs.
Nouns: **robber,** person who **robs,** normally with violence or the threat of violence; **robbery,** usually on a large scale, using weapons.
Problem: They've **robbed** the bank. (**NOT** stolen)

steal (stole, stolen)
2 *He* **stole** *the money/the ring.*
4 *He* **stole** *a lot of money* **from** *us.*

See **rob.**
Nouns: note that the equivalents to **robber** and **robbery** for people who **steal** and their actions are **thief, theft.**
Problems:
They've **stolen** my money. (**NOT** robbed)
They've **stolen** a lot of things **from** us. (**NOT** They've stolen/robbed us a lot of things)

Complete the sentences, using the correct verb in the appropriate form. Pay attention to the structure.

1 Robin Hood is a folk hero who is supposed to have _____ the rich and _____ their money to give it to the poor.
2 I've been _____! My purse has been _____!
3 We know that you _____ the money from the bank. We have witnesses who saw you _____ the bank and escape with the money.
4 Have you ever been _____?
   Well, yes. I had my watch _____ once, but I wasn't really _____, because I left it in the changing-room in my club.
   All the same, someone _____ it.
   Yes, though it's not the same as being mugged and _____ of everything you are carrying. Somehow, if something is _____ from the place where you leave it, it's not so bad as when you are _____ personally and cannot prevent it.

21 say, speak, talk, tell

	1	2	3	4	7	12	19	20	21	22	27
	−O	O	PO	2O	OI	TH	SO	OTH	OQW	OQWI	OSO
say (to 3,4)	×	×	×	×		×	×				
speak (to 3)	×	×	×								
talk (to 3)	×	×	×								
tell	×	×	×	×	×			×	×	×	×

say (said, said)
1 *It goes without* saying *– that is to say, I think so anyway – that . . .*
2 *He* said *some interesting things at the party.*
3 *'You're looking well,' I* said *to him.*
4 *He didn't* say *anything to me about it.*
12 *He* said *that he would be late this evening.*
19 *How do you know it's true?*
    My mother said *so.*

We **say** words (**to** people); we **tell** people information. So we can write, 'Hello!' she **said** (**to** me)', but could not use **tell** because 'Hello' is not information.
Noun: **saying**, well-known phrase.
Problem: What did he **say to** you? (**NOT** say you)

speak (spoke, spoken)
1 *No one* spoke. *(No one* said *anything.)*
2 *Can you* speak *French?*
3 *He hasn't* spoken *to me for days.*

Speak means 'say things' (1). It is often interchangeable with **talk**, but the implication of **talk** is to have a conversation with someone. Compare 'Who was **speaking**?' and 'What were they **talking** about?'
Noun: **speech**, formal statement in public ('make a **speech**'), or the power of **speaking**.
Problems:
Is there anyone who **speaks** Russian? (**NOT** talks)
He didn't want to **speak to** me. (**NOT** speak me)

talk
1 *Can the bird* talk?
2 *You're* talking *nonsense.*
3 *You should* talk *to your guests.*

Note that in example **1**, the point is that birds make sounds, but only a few birds, like parrots, imitate human conversation. See **speak**, above.
Noun: **talk**, conversation or an informal lecture.

tell (told, told)
1 *Who will win? I can't* **tell** *(I don't know).*
2 *You're not* **telling** *the truth.*
3 **Tell** *me! What happened?*
4 *He didn't* **tell** *me anything about it.*
7 **Tell** *them to come in.*
20 *They* **told** *us that we would have to wait.*
21 *Can you* **tell** *me where the station is.*
22 *I've* **told** *them where to go.*
27 *I was right, after all. I* **told** *you so.*

For the basic meaning, see **say.** Note that **tell** is used with a personal object without 'to'. It is used in indirect commands (7).

Tell exists in a number of phrases – '**tell** the truth', '**tell** lies', etc., and also has different meanings in some contexts: '**tell** the time', understand a clock; '**tell** a story', relate.

Problems:
Who **told** you to do that? (**NOT** said/told to)
Who **told** you where I was? (**NOT** said)
Who **told** you what to do? (**NOT** said)

Complete the sentences, using the correct verb in the appropriate form. Pay special attention to the structure, but also note the meaning in the context and any phrases you have heard or seen.

1 Did you _____?
  No, I didn't _____ anything.
  I thought you were trying to _____ me something.
2 The police have been _____ about it, and I can _____ you this. If you don't stop _____ nonsense, and _____ me the truth, you'll be sorry.
3 'He's only four. He doesn't know how to _____ the time yet,' she _____.
4 The teacher _____ the children not to _____ in class.
5 Of course we should have _____ you – it goes without _____ that we rely on your co-operation.
  I expected you to _____ that. But I think you didn't want to _____ anything to me because I warned you of what might happen, and you were afraid I would _____ 'I _____ you so'.
6 He can _____ several languages. The trouble is, he hasn't anything interesting to _____ in any of them.
7 They'll do the job provided you _____ them what to do. Perhaps we can _____ about it after the meeting tomorrow.
8 'You shouldn't smoke so much', he _____ to me. As he had never _____ to me before in my life, I _____ him to mind his own business.
9 It _____ in the paper that we shall have fine weather this summer.
  Oh well, if the paper _____ so, let's hope they're right, but I doubt if they can _____ us when to go on holiday.
10 _____ me! Have I done anything to upset you? We always used to _____ to each other quite naturally, but you haven't _____ a word to me for the last three days.

SECTION TWO

22 accept, admit, agree, approve

	1	2	3	5	6	12	26
	−O	O	PO	I	G	TH	OAS
accept	×	×	×			×	×
admit		×	×		×	×	×
agree (on, to 2; with 2,3)	×	×	×	×		×	
approve (of 2,3)	×	×	×				

accept
1 *It's a good offer. I* **accept** *(it).*
2 *I'm afraid I can't* **accept** *a cheque. The company doesn't allow it.*
3 *The club* **accepted** *him (as a member).*
12 *I* **accept** *that we should have warned you about this.*
26 *He was* **accepted** *as a member of the club.*

Accept means to 'receive willingly' but can also mean **agree to** (2) and **admit** (12), though it does not imply guilt.
Noun: **acceptance.**

admit (admitted, admitted)
2 *He* **admitted** *his mistake.*
3 *This pass* **admits** *two people to the theatre.*
6 *Do you* **admit** *(to) having stolen the car?*
12 *He* **admitted** *that he had taken it.*
26 *He was* **admitted** *(to the club) as a member.* (This is more formal in implication than **accepted**, in example **26**.)

Admit means 'confess' (2), (6), (12) and 'allow to enter' (3), (26), where it has a personal object.
Nouns: **admittance,** entrance – 'No **admittance** to unauthorised persons'; **admission,** confession or the price of entering – '**admission** fees'.

agree (agreed, agreed)
1 *A good idea! I* **agree.**
2 *I* **agree to** *your proposal. Go ahead!*
I **agree with** *your idea. I think it will work.*
We **agree on** *most points, but not entirely.*
3 *I don't* **agree with** *you. I think you're mistaken.*
5 *They* **agreed** *to come with us.*
16 *I* **agree** *that it's a bad time to go on holiday.*

Agree means 'to have the same opinion' (1), (2 with, on), (3 with), (12); 'to accept, because you **approve of** something' (2 to), (5). **Agree to** implies more freedom of

choice than **accept**, and probably greater responsibility.
Noun: **agreement**, having the same opinion, or a formal promise (i.e. between countries, companies, etc.)
Problem: They **agreed** to come with us. (**NOT** accepted)

approve (approved, approved)
1 *Do you think they will* **approve** (*of the marriage*)?
2 *I don't* **approve of** *that sort of behaviour.*
3 *My parents-in-law don't* **approve of** *me.*

Approve means 'to consider people, things or actions good or right'; it takes **of** when followed by an object.
Noun: **approval**, which in some cases can mean 'permission', but usually applies to the state of mind.
Problem: They have **passed** their exams. (**NOT** approved)

Complete the sentences, using the correct verb in the appropriate tense. Consider the meaning and the structure.

1 We _____ to give him a month's trial in the firm, but he did not _____ our conditions.
2 I am pleased to _____ your kind invitation.
3 I never expected him to _____ the crime; apparently, he _____ with his lawyer that it would be wiser to do so.
4 The club did not _____ (*or* _____) him as a member because they did not _____ of his behaviour.
5 He has _____ taking the money, but I think we should give him another chance. Do you _____?
6 No one under 18 is _____ to this show.
7 We don't _____ all the conditions in the contract, but we _____ on the main points.
8 I _____ with his ideas, but I don't _____ of his behaviour.

23 ache, damage, harm, hurt, injure, wound

	1	2	11	associations
	−O	O	R	
ache	×			slow pain, headache, etc.
damage		×		objects, not people
harm		×		wrong, physical or mental
hurt	×	×	×	
injure		×		accident
wound		×		battle

ache (ached, ached)
1   *My head* aches.

Ache suggests the pain continues – **headache, toothache, back ache,** and **stomach ache** are the most common nouns derived from it.
Nouns: all the nouns for these verbs are practised in Part A, Unit 17.

damage (damaged, damaged)
2   *The building was* **damaged** *in the storm.*

Note the association with objects and avoid using this verb for people; see **injure, wound.**
Noun: **damage** (uncountable).

harm
2   *The dog won't* **harm** *you. (The dog won't* **do you** *any* **harm** *is more common and less formal.)*

Noun: **harm.**

hurt (hurt, hurt)
1   *Ow! That* **hurts!**
2   *Let go of my arm! You're* **hurting** *me.*
     Their unkindness **hurt** *her terribly.*
11   *Don't climb up there! You'll* **hurt** *yourself!*

Hurt is the most common verb, with the widest range of usage. It is preferable to **ache** when the pain is sharp (1). It can be used for emotional as well as physical pain (2). **Injure** and **wound** are more specific – see below.
Noun: **hurt,** but this is seldom used, and in different contexts, we would usually say **pain, injury** or **harm.**
Problem: This won't do you any **harm.** (**NOT** hurt)

injure (injured, injured)
2   *They were seriously* **injured** *in a car accident.*

Hurt is often used instead of **injure,** but **injure** tends to emphasise the seriousness of what happens, and an **injured** person would always require medical treatment. Emotionally, the word is formal, and often sounds false; **hurt** is preferable.
Noun: **injury,** serious **harm** to the body, also to your pride, reputation, etc., when it is very formal.
Problem: He was **injured** in the accident. (**NOT** damaged/wounded)

wound
2   *The police shot and* **wounded** *him when he tried to escape.*

Wound is used for **injuries,** especially those sustained in war from a bullet, sword, etc., but you must be a combatant to be **wounded;** a person in a house hit by a bomb would be **injured.** It can be used figuratively of people whose feelings are badly **hurt,** but it is wiser to avoid it.
Noun: **wound,** also applied to deep cuts, whether or not they occured in the war.
Problem: He was **wounded** in the battle. (**NOT** damaged)

Complete the sentences, using the most suitable verb in the appropriate form. Consider the meaning in the context as well as the structure.

1 The bomb fell near the hospital, _____ several buildings nearby. A number of civilians were _____ and taken to hospital, and some soldiers who were _____ in the battle outside the town last week were cut by flying glass.

2 This shouldn't _____, because I'm going to give you an injection, but you may find that the tooth starts _____ when you get home, so I'll give you some aspirins. Two aspirins won't _____ you (or _____ you any _____).

3 Don't try to lift that heavy case. You'll _____ (or _____) yourself.

4 When the fans ran onto the pitch, the main stand was _____ and several policemen were _____ (or _____).

5 She was _____ when the boss spoke to her so unkindly.

24 achieve, manage, succeed

	1	2	5	6
	−O	O	I	G
achieve		×		
manage (to 5)	×	×	×	
succeed (to 2, in 6)	×	×		×

achieve (achieved, achieved)
2 *He has* **achieved** *his aims in life.*

Achieve means 'to gain as a result of action', but it tends to be used with abstract nouns – compare: 'He has won a prize/He got good marks in the exam'.
Noun: **achievement**, gaining something or what is gained, with the implications of skill, hard work, moral value, not for example money, popularity.

manage (managed, managed)
1 *You needn't help me. I can* **manage**.
2 *He* **manages** *a hotel on the Costa Brava.*
5 *Some of the sailors were drowned, but he* **managed** *to reach to shore.*

Manage means '**succeed in** dealing with something' (1), (5), or 'be in charge of, control' (2).
The main problem with **manage** and **succeed** (compare **succeed** in example 6) lies in the forms, and their relationship to 'could' and 'was able to'. In past time, when an action involves overcoming difficulties by a person's own efforts, 'could' cannot be used. Compare the following: 'If he can/is able to/**manages to** obtain a loan from the bank, his problems will be solved.' and 'The others were drowned, but he was a good swimmer and was able to/**managed to** reach the shore.'
Nouns: **manager**; **management**, the act of **managing** a business or a group of people in charge of a firm, considered together as '**Management** and workers'.
Problem: See example above where 'could' is not correct.

110

succeed

1 *He set out to win the prize, and he* **succeeded**.
2 *When his brother died, he* **succeeded** *him as king.*
6 *Some of the sailors were drowned, but he* **succeeded** *in reaching the shore.*

Succeed is the opposite of 'fail' (**1**), and also has the meaning of 'follow in an official position' or 'take over an official position' (**2**). Where **succeed in** is equivalent to **manage to** (**6**), the difference is in the form. Compare the following to the example for **manage to** given above:
If he **succeeds in** obtaining a loan from the bank, his problems will be solved.
See example given for **6** above, and compare.
Nouns: **success**, the act of **succeeding**, a person or thing that **succeeds**; **succession**, the act of following; **successor**, person who **succeeds** another in an official position.
Problem: The accident **occurred** at three o'clock. (**NOT** succeeded)

Complete the sentences, using the correct verb in the appropriate form. Pay special attention to the structure, but also consider the meaning.

1 I'm glad you _____ to pass the exam. That will help you to _____ your aims.
2 He found it difficult to _____ such a large firm at first, but now he has _____ in solving the main problems and can look forward to _____ his objectives.
3 Mr Noel Andrews has been appointed to _____ Mr Allan Cunningham as Headmaster. His aim is to maintain the high levels the school has already _____.
4 When he took on this new job he seemed bound to _____, but now his expenses have risen so much that he is finding it hard to _____.
5 At first I found it difficult to persuade the students to do some work at home, but I eventually _____ in demonstrating to them how important it was. Once I had _____ to do that, their results were excellent.

25 advertise, advise, announce, threaten, warn

	1	2	3	4	5	6	7	12	20
	–O	O	PO	2O	I	G	OI	TH	OTH
advertise (for 3)	×	×	×					×	
advise (on 4)	(×)	×	×	×		×	×		×
announce (to 4)		×	(×)	×				×	
threaten (with 4)	×	×	×	×	×				
warn (of, against 4)	(×)		×	×			×	×	×

advertise (advertised, advertised)
1 Do you **advertise** *(your products) in the newspaper?*
2 *We* **advertised** *the job in the newspaper yesterday.*

3 *We have* **advertised for** *a secretary.*
12 *They* **advertised** *that they would sell the goods at half-price.*

To **advertise** is to draw (people's) attention to something, usually in the newspaper, on TV, etc. We **advertise** what is available (2), but **advertise for** what we want (3).
Nouns: **advertising**, in general; **advertisement**, in particular.
Problem: They've **advertised** their new product on TV. (**NOT** announced)

advise (advised, advised)

1 *I'm only here to* **advise** *(you). I can't tell you what to do.*
2 *I don't* **advise** *any action at this moment.*
3 *Your lawyer is present to* **advise** *you.*
4 *He* **advised** *the managing director* **on** *legal matters.*
6 *I* **advise** *taking no further action until we hear from their lawyers.*
7 *I* **advise** *you to keep silent under the circumstances.*
20 *They* **advised** *us that it would be sensible to stay indoors until the political situation was clearer.*

To **advise** is to say to/tell people what should be done. In **4**, note that we **advise** people **on** subjects. The word always suggests authority, and is used in formal contexts, where the person **advising** is for example a lawyer, a doctor, or, in **20**, the consulate. A less formal means of expressing this is 'take/give **advice**': 'If you take my **advice**, you won't do it'.
Noun: **advice** (uncountable). Note 'a piece of **advice**' for a particular suggestion.
Problem: We were **told/informed** that they would not be coming. (**NOT** 'advised', except in very formal circumstances.)

announce (announced, announced)

2 *British Airways* **announce** *the departure of Flight 123.*
3 *The guests at the Royal Garden Party were* **announced** *when they arrived.*
4 *They* **announced** *the news* **to** *the waiting crowd outside.*
12 *They* **announced** *that they were getting married.*

Announce is 'to say something, give information in public'. We **announce** information **to** those who are listening (4). In a special case (3), it means 'say the guests' names' so that those present will know who they are.
Nouns: **announcement**; **announcer**, person who reads the news on TV, for example.
Problem: They've just **announced** that the flight will be delayed. (**NOT** advised/ noticed)

threaten

1 *Danger* **threatens.**
2 *Those clouds* **threaten** *rain.*
3 *Are you* **threatening** *me?*
4 *He was* **threatened with** *severe punishment.*
5 *He* **threatened** *to hit me.*

Threaten is to say/tell people that you will do something bad to them (3) (4), (5). Note that we **threaten** people **with** the action (4). In **1** and **2**, the idea is of something bad likely to happen.
Noun: **threat**, expressing the intention to do something bad or disagreeable.

warn

1 'Prime Minister **warns**'
3 I **warned** you. Now the responsibility is yours.
4 I've **warned** them **of** the risks involved.
   I **warned** him **against** (trusting) them.
7 We **warned** them not to play near the edge of the cliff.
12/20 They **warned** (us) that what we were planning to do was dangerous.

Warn means 'to point out (to people) the bad or dangerous consequences of their actions for their own good'. In the special case of **1**, which is newspaper jargon, the meaning is close to **threaten** (**1**).
Noun: **warning** – e.g. 'air raid **warning**', gale **warning**'.
Problem: I **warned** you that the plan might fail. (**NOT** advertised/advised)

Complete the sentences, using the correct verb in the appropriate form. Consider the meaning and the structure.

1 They've _____ for a secretary but so far no one has applied for the job.
2 We _____ the children not to cross the main road except at the traffic lights.
3 They _____ on the TV news last night that the police have _____ (or _____) the Prime Minister not to _____ public appearances in advance because someone has _____ to kill him.
4 The judge _____ him of the consequences if he broke the law again and _____ him with a prison sentence if he did not take his advice.
5 Mr Jonathan Charles has been appointed to _____ the company on legal matters. The Managing Director _____ the appointment to the Board yesterday.
6 Cigarette companies are not allowed to _____ their products on TV, and the packets must carry an announcement _____ smokers of the risks to their health.
7 'I _____ you that if you don't get out of my office immediately, you'll be sorry.'
   'Are you _____ me?'
   'I'm not going to hit you, if that's what you mean, but I have lawyers to _____ me, and they will tell me what to do.'
8 The Minister _____ in Parliament yesterday that the claims made for these products when they were _____ on TV were false. Doctors had been instructed to _____ their patients against them. The Minister _____ chemists who sold them with prosecution.

26 aid, assist, help, can't help, support

	1	2	5	6	7	associations
	−O	O	I	G	OI	
aid		×				a country, a group
assist		×			×	another worker (assistant)
help	×	×	×		×	
can't help		×		×		
support		×				

aid
2 *The rich countries should* **aid** *the poorer ones.*

Aid means 'help', but is almost always used formally for official projects.
Noun: **aid,** to third-world countries, to the Red Cross.
Problem: **Help** me! (**NOT** Aid me!)

assist
2 *I've been* **assisting** *Dr Taylor (***in/with** *his research).*
7 *The machine has been designed to* **assist** *patients who have breathing problems to breathe more easily.*

Assist also means '**help**'. It is used in formal contexts when both sides must contribute to the result – i.e. in examples 7, the machine cannot breathe for the patients.
Nouns: **assistance; assistant.**
Problem: I **attended/was present at** the meeting last week. (**NOT** assisted at)

help
1 *Making jokes doesn't* **help** *in this situation.*
2 **Help** *me! I'm drowning!*
5 **Help** *(to) carry the luggage upstairs, will you?*
7 *She* **helped** *her mother (to) cook the dinner.*

Help (1) means 'make things better'. Note that with the infinitive constructions (5), (7), **help** is found with and without 'to'.
Noun: **help.**

can't help
2 *I* **can't help** *it. It's not my fault.*
6 *I know he's all right, but I* **can't help** *worrying about him.*

Can't help means 'can't avoid'.

support
2 *Do you earn enough to* **support** *your family?*
Which team do you **support**?
If you propose this change in the law, I will **support** *you/it.*

Support means, in the examples given, 'provide for' a family, 'take an active interest in' a team, 'actively help' a person or 'be in favour of' a proposal.
Nouns: **support**, help, encouragement; **supporter**, one who favours a policy or team.
Problems:
I can't **stand**/can't **bear** rats. (**NOT** support)
I don't know how you can **put up with** him/his behaviour. He's so rude! (**NOT** support)

Complete the sentences, using the correct verb in the appropriate form. Consider the meaning and the context, as well as the structure. Use **aid** or **assist** rather than **help** where the context seems appropriate.

1 Good morning. Can I _____ you?
2 Perhaps you _____ wondering why the person who says that is called a 'shop assistant'. It may _____ you to look at the examples again, but it's really because the English like Latin words for official titles.
3 Obviously we have a duty to _____ developing countries, and I will _____ any policy with that intention.
4 'I still _____ the team although I don't go to the matches. I _____ feeling happy when I see that it's won.'
'But you're not _____ the team's efforts to survive by staying away.'
'I _____ that. The other 'supporters' are too violent, and I can't stand violence.'
5 I've been _____ the Mayor in drawing up a programme to _____ those who haven't enough money to _____ their families.

27 appoint, choose, elect, pick

	1	2	5	7	24	26	associations
	−O	O	I	OI	ONC	OAS	
appoint		×		×	×	×	business, civil service
choose	×	×	×	×		×	
elect		×		×	×	×	politics, voting
pick		×		×		×	sport, team

appoint
2 *They've* **appointed** *a new head teacher.*
7 *The government has* **appointed** *him (to be) ambassador to the United Nations.*
24 *They* **appointed** *him headmaster.*
26 *They* **appointed** *him as Chairman of the committee.*

Appoint, like **elect** and **pick**, is used as a variant of **choose** in certain contexts. It means 'choose someone for a job, public position'. Constructions 7, 24 and 26 are interchangeable; 26 is probably the least common. People are **appointed to** posts.
Noun: **appointment**, post, time when you arrange to meet someone, 'dental **appointment**'.
Problem: She **noted down** what the teacher said. (**NOT** appointed)

choose (chose, chosen)

1 *It's your decision! You* **choose***!*
2 *I* **chose** *a tie to go with my new suit.*
5 *Why did you* **choose** *to stay behind?*
7 *She has been* **chosen** *to make a speech welcoming the visitors to the school.*
26 *They* **chose** *her* **as** *the school's representative.*

Choose can mean 'decide' (**1**), (**5**). Note that we **choose between** alternatives, **choose from** a number of possibilities.
People are **chosen for** positions, responsibilities.
Noun: **choice**, act of **choosing** – 'make your **choice**', the right to **choose**, person/thing **chosen**, or the variety of things to **choose** from.

elect

2 *They've* **elected** *a new government.*
7 *They* **elected** *him to represent them.*
24 *They* **elected** *him president.*
26 *They* **elected** *him* **as** *their president for life.*

Elect means '**choose** by voting' (see associations in the chart). The constructions are the same as for **appoint**, and **26** is less common than **7** and **24**; the difference is the method used to **choose** the person.
People are **elected to** positions.
Nouns: **election** – 'General **Election**'; **elector**, voter.
Problem: She **chose** the blue dress. (**NOT** elected)

pick

2 *They've* **picked** *a different team for tomorrow's game.*
7 *He was* **picked** *to play for England.*
26 *We* **picked** *him from the short list as the obvious candidate for the job.*

Pick has many other meanings, for example, '**pick** flowers', '**pick up** a book from the floor'. It implies careful selection, **choosing** between rival candidates, in the examples above, but is also used for betting, gambling – 'She **picked** the winner'. Note in example **26**, that the candidate would first be **picked** (**chosen**) and then **appointed** (offered the job).
Noun: **pick**, 'Take your **pick**' = '**choice**', but is less formal.
Problem: The bee **stung** me. (**NOT** picked)

Complete the sentences, using the most suitable verb in the context, in the appropriate form. Consider the meaning, the context and the structure. Only use **choose** when it is necessary.

1 He won a prize because he _____ the winning number out of a hat.
2 Now that the government has been _____, the Prime Minister is expected to _____ James Cross as Home Secretary.
3 It's important for me to _____ the best team to play on Saturday but it's difficult to _____ between Jack and Andrew in goal.
4 The government wanted to _____ her to represent the country at the United Nations, but she _____ to remain at the university.
5 The secret of _____ the right people to parliament is to _____ good candidates to represent the party at the election.

6 What a coincidence! We've just _____ Richard Smith as headmaster and now
   the teacher's union have voted for local representatives and _____ his brother
   to negotiate with him.

28 arise, raise, rise

	1	2	11	associations
	−O	O	R	
arise	×			difficulty, trouble
raise		×	×	doubt, price, subject
rise	×			price, sun, smoke, temperature

arise (arose, arisen)
1 *All kinds of problems have* **arisen** *since you left.*

Arise means to appear, happen, present itself, 'come up', but is seldom used except
with the associations listed.

raised (**raised**, **raised**, present participle, **raising**)
2 *He* **raised** *his hand, asking for silence.*
   My landlady has **raised** *my rent.*
11 *He* **raised himself** *on his elbows, and looked around.*

Raise is regular, and always has an object. It means 'lift, put up, cause to go up' and in
some cases, for example **raise** a subject, 'bring up'.
Problems:
He **raised** (put up) his hand. (**NOT** rose/got up)
He **gets up** early every day. (**NOT** raises himself)

rise (rose, risen, present participle, **rising**)
1 *What time does the sun* **rise** *tomorrow?*
   Prices have **risen** *(gone up).*
   The temperature is **rising**.

Rise is irregular (see **raise**) and never has an object. It means 'come up' or 'go up', and
also 'get up', but here it is very formal – 'He **rose** early'.
Problems:
Prices are **rising**. (**NOT** raising)
But note: They have **raised** their prices. (**NOT** risen)

Complete the sentences, using the correct verb in the appropriate form. Consider the
structure but also take the meaning into account.

1 When he _____ to address Parliament there was so much noise that he had to
   _____ his hand to ask for silence.
2 A number of problems have _____ in the factory, largely because the firm has
   refused to _____ the workers' wages.

3 The Government _____ the hopes of the electorate by saying that prices would not _____ after the election.
4 If we feel compelled to _____ objections to the Government's action, it is because they have lied to the people. If they had told the truth these problems would not have _____.
5 He _____ himself to his full height.

---

29 ask, ask for, claim, demand, insist

	1	2	4	5	6	7	8	12	21	22
	-O	O	2O	I	G	OI	OG	TH	OQW	OQWI
ask		×	×	×		×		×	×	×
ask for		×	×							
claim		×		×				×		
demand		×		×				×		
insist (on 2,6,8)	×	×			×		×	×		

ask
2 I asked *a question, but you haven't answered.*
4 They asked *him his name.*
5 He asked *to go out, but he wasn't allowed to leave.*
7 Ask *him to come in.*
12 He asked *that other crimes should be taken into consideration.*
21 Ask *him what he wants.*
22 Ask *him what to do.*

We ask (people) questions in order to get information (2), (4), (21), (22); alternatively, the verb means that we would like people to do things for us, give permission (5), (7), (12). In contrast, we ask for information, help, services, etc. or objects.
Problems:
I asked him his name. (NOT demanded)
I asked the teacher a question. (NOT asked to)

ask for
2 He asked for *my advice.*
4 We asked *them* for *some money.*

See ask.
Problem: I asked him for the money. (NOT I asked him the money)

claim
2 She claimed *her rights according to the law.*
5 He claims *to be the nephew of the Duke of Essex.*
12 He claimed *that he had never seen the witness before.*

118

To **claim** is 'to say something belongs to you' (**2**), or 'say something is true'. In this sense, it can mean **ask for**, but is more formal, with legal implications.
Noun: **claim**, demand that something belongs to you by right, statement that something is true, the right to something – 'He has a **claim** on us/to our sympathy'.
Problem: I **claimed** the insurance on the house. (**NOT** 'reclaimed' which means 'claimed again or recovered'.)

demand
2 I **demand** *an explanation.*
5 *She* **demanded** *to see the manager.*
12 *He* **demanded** *that they should listen to his complaints.*

Demand means '**ask for** something and not accept 'no' for an answer' or '**claim** as a right'. It is usually more formal than **ask for** because of the possible legal implications.
Noun: **demand**, the act of demanding or people's desire for goods or services, willingness to pay for them – 'This product is **in demand**' (frequently asked for).
Problem: I **demand** an explanation. (**NOT** I ask)

insist
1 *Of course you can see the manager, if you* **insist.**
2 *He* **insisted on** *his rights.*
6 *I* **insist on** *seeing her.*
8 *I* **insist on** *them coming here immediately.*
12 *I* **insisted** *that they should be properly treated.*

Insist (**on** something) is to **ask for**, **demand** or **claim** it repeatedly, not accepting 'no' for an answer.
Noun: **insistence.**
Problem: I **insist on** seeing the manager. (**NOT** persist in/insist to see)

Complete the sentences, using the correct verb in the appropriate form. Consider the structure and the meaning.

1 I _____ a friend of mine to help me.
   I _____ his help.
2 They _____ the money in loud voices, _____ that it belonged to them. Although they _____, I refused to pay them unless they _____ it in a civilised manner.
3 If you _____ to be the son of a duke, why are you _____ me to lend you money?
4 You have a right to _____ me questions, but you have no right to _____ an answer. If you _____ on making a nuisance of yourself, I will _____ you to leave.
5 _____ her where she lives and how to get in touch with her. She _____ that she knows where the money is hidden, but she _____ on us keeping it a secret.
6 We _____ them _____ some money, but they _____ to see our passports before they would give it to us.
7 He _____ on seeing you.
   Well, _____ him his name, and if I know him, _____ him to come in.
8 He _____ his rights as a citizen, and _____ to see a lawyer.
   Oh, well, if he _____ on it, let him ring his lawyer.

30 avoid, escape, hinder, prevent, stop

	1	2	6	8	17
	–O	O	G	OG	VC
avoid		×	×		
escape (from 2)	×	×			
hinder		×			
prevent (from 8)		×		×	
stop	×	×	×	×	×

avoid
2 *He agreed in order to* **avoid** *trouble.*
6 *She* **avoided** *answering my question.*

Avoid means 'to keep away from', usually by taking deliberate previous action – you **avoid** an accident by driving well. In the same way you **avoid** a person you do not want to meet by going in a different direction. See **escape.**
Noun: **avoidance.**
Problem: I **avoided** meeting him. (**NOT** avoided to meet him)

escape (escaped, escaped)
1 *The prisoners have* **escaped.**
2 *They* **escaped from** *prison/the police.*
  They were lucky to **escape** *death.*

Escape means 'to get out' (**1**) or 'get away from' (**2**), (with **from**), but also 'not to suffer something bad (**2**). It is much more active in implication than **avoid** and involves action taken afterwards, not before, in the first two examples.
Noun: **escape,** the act of **escaping** or just managing to **avoid** something bad – 'a narrow **escape**'.
Problem: They **escaped from** the police in a stolen car. (**NOT** 'avoided the police' in this context.)

hinder
2 *You're* **hindering** *my work by talking so much.*
  Her long skirts **hindered** *her when she jumped off the bus.*

Hinder means to partly prevent, or prevent the completion of something. It is normally used in everyday contexts, where the consequences are not very serious.
Noun: **hindrance,** something or someone that gets in the way.

prevent
2 *How can we* **prevent** *war?*
8 *The rain* **prevented** *them (from) playing.*

Prevent means 'do something so that something does not happen'.
Noun: **prevention** – '**prevention** of cruelty to animals'.

Problems:
The rain **prevented** them from playing. (**NOT** avoided)
They **foresaw** the difficulties involved, and so they cancelled the trip. (**NOT** prevented)

stop (stopped, stopped)
1 *I'm glad the rain has* **stopped**.
2 *Why didn't the referee* **stop** *the fight?*
6 *They* **stopped** *arguing and listened to her.*
8 *I can't* **stop** *you going out if you want to.*
17 *If you don't want to come with us,* **stop** *(stay) at home all evening.*

Stop is equivalent to **prevent** in **8**, but elsewhere means 'not continue' (**1**), (**6**), 'end' (**2**), or 'stay' (**17**). Note that 'he **stopped** talking' (**6**), means 'he became silent', but 'he **stopped** to talk to her', means he **stopped** (**1**) (for example walking) because he wanted to talk to her.
Nouns: **stop** – 'bus **stop**', 'full **stop**'; **stoppage**, hold-up in work; **stopper**, top of bottle, replaceable after use.

Complete the sentences, using the correct verb in the appropriate form. Pay special attention to the meaning in context, as well as the structure.

1 We were lucky to _____ an accident. It was only Jack's prompt action in braking sharply that _____ us from crashing into the back of the other car.
2 Britain's most wanted criminal, Richard Turpin, _____ from Albany Prison yesterday. Road blocks have been set up to _____ (*or* _____) him leaving the country.
3 He's always _____ me in my work by talking to me but it's difficult to _____ answering him when we are in the same room, and once he starts talking, he never _____.
4 People who work for a monthly salary can hardly _____ paying taxes. The firm takes the money from them before they are paid so they can't _____. Tax inspectors are mainly concerned with people who _____ taxation because they work for themselves and can arrange their bills. They are doing what they can to _____ (*or* _____) this, but the lack of sympathy most people have for them _____ them.
5 The referee has _____ the game because Walker is injured.
6 He really ought to _____ playing football. He's too old, and he's been lucky to _____ serious injury up to now, but nothing I say will _____ him from playing. He says he doesn't want to _____ at home every Saturday watching the television.

31 bend, fold, wind, wrap

	1	2	associations
	−O	O	
bend (down 1)	×	×	1 road; 2 your knees, wire
fold (up 1,2)	(×)	×	1 table; 2 cloth, paper, your arms
wind (up 2)	×	×	1 river, path; 2 handle, watch
wrap (up 1,2)	(×)	×	1 yourself; 2 parcel

bend (bent, bent)
1 *Slow down when the road* **bends** *sharply.*
  He **bent down** *and picked up the paper.*
2 *He* **bent** *the wire until the ends touched.*
  I hate going round old castles, and having to **bend** *my head every time I go through a doorway.*

Bend suggests a more abrupt and complete movement than 'curve' (see first example of **2**). It is also more commonly used except in, for example, geometry. The difference is clearly indicated by the nouns: a road climbing a mountain (*Fig. 1*) consists of a series of 'hairpin **bends**'; any part of a circle forms a 'curve'.

Fig. 1

Noun: **bend,** in the road.
Problem: He **bent down** and picked up the paper. (**NOT** curved)

fold
1 *Does this table* **fold** *(up)?*
2 **Fold** *the letter and put it in the envelope.*

Fold implies that surfaces touch; if you '**fold** your arms' you cross them over your chest.
Noun: **fold,** in a skirt, curtain.
Problem: **Fold** the letter and put it in the envelope. (**NOT** bend)
Note that we say 'Do not **bend** photographs'. It would obviously ruin them to **fold** them.

wind (wound, wound)
1 *The river* **winds** *through the forest.*
2 *I haven't* **wound** *(up) my watch.*

Wind implies changes of direction (**1**), (*Fig. 2*) or circular revolutions (**2**). It rhymes with 'mind'; and the past tense rhymes with 'sound'.

Fig. 2

wrap (wrapped, wrapped)
1 **Wrap up** *warmly. It's a cold day.*
2 **Wrap** *it (up) in a parcel and post it.*

Wrap suggests 'cover, **fold** round', so in **1** 'wrap up' means 'put on a scarf, overcoat, etc.'
Noun: **wrapping**, paper around parcels, presents, etc. – 'wrapping paper'.

Complete the sentences, using the correct verb in the appropriate form. Consider the associations as well as the general meaning.

1 He _____ down to pick up the paper he had dropped.
2 _____ the letter and put it in the envelope. I'll _____ up this parcel and you can take them both to the Post Office.
3 He was strong enough to _____ thick iron bars.
4 I must _____ up my watch. It's stopped.
5 You should _____ your knees as the ball comes towards you. Don't just stand there with your arms _____.
6 The road _____ sharply, following the course of the river as it _____ through the mountains.

32 check, control, look over, look through, revise

	1	2	11	12	13	14
	−O	O	R	TH	QW	QWI
check	×	×		×	×	×
control		×	×			
look over		×				
look through		×				
revise	×	×				

check
1   *I think we sent off the order, but I'll* **check.**
2   *I* **checked** *my shopping list before going out.*
12 *Before you go out,* **check** *that the windows are closed.*
13/14 *I want to look at the map to* **check** *where we leave/where to leave the motorway.*

Check means 'look (at something) to make sure it is correct'.
Noun: **check,** examination to see things are all right; **check-up,** medical examination (**NOT** revision).
Problems:
The ticket collector **checked** my ticket. (**NOT** controlled)
The mechanic is **checking/overhauling** my car. (**NOT** revising)

control (controlled, controlled)
2 *You should* **control** *your temper.*
11 **Control** *yourself! Don't get so excited.*

Control is 'to have power over' or 'keep under **control'.**
Noun: **control,** political **control** over a country, etc.; **control** tower, at an airport, **controlling** flights.

look over
2 *Would you mind* **looking over** *this letter to make sure I haven't missed anything out?*

Look over is 'to examine quickly', whereas **look through** implies examining in greater detail, reading but not reading every word.
Problem: He **looked over** my work. (**NOT** 'overlooked', which means 'forgot to pay attention to'.)

look through
2 *I haven't read the book, but I* **looked through** *it and it seems interesting.*

See **look over.**

revise (revised, revised)

1 *I have to* **revise** *for my exams.*
2 *We shall have to* **revise** *the book and make a few changes before we publish a new edition.*

Revise is 'to go over notes' (**1**) or 'to make necessary alterations to' a plan, book, etc.(**2**).
Noun: **revision**, preparation for examinations (uncountable), alterations to a book (can be countable).
Problems:
They have **reviewed** the film in the newspaper (= written a report on it). (**NOT** revised)
The mechanic is **overhauling** my car. (**NOT** revising)

Complete the sentences, using the correct verb in the appropriate form. Consider the meaning as well as the structure. Do not use the same verb twice in the same sentence.

1 I agree that the firm is spending too much and we must _____ this expenditure, but before we _____ the system so that everyone has to learn a new procedure, we should _____ that the findings in this report are correct.
2 I've reviewed the book for tomorrow's paper, but I want to _____ what I have written to _____ a few details.
3 I'm _____ for the exam. First, I'm going to _____ my essays carefully, and then I must _____ whether I missed something important on the days when I was away.
4 You should _____ yourself in public. I used to think you were a calm person, but I've _____ my opinion.
5 We were in such a hurry that I didn't have time to _____ the order carefully. I just _____ the list and everything seemed to be all right, so I sent it off.

33 consider, realise, think about, think of, understand

	1	2	6	7	9	12	13	14	23	24
	−O	O	G	OI	OP	TH	QW	QWI	OAC	ONC
consider	(×)	×	×	(×)		(×)	(×)	(×)	×	×
realise		×				×	×			
think about		×	×		×		×	×		
think of		×	×		×		×	×		
understand	×	×		(×)		×	×	×		

consider
1 *He paused for a moment to* **consider** *(think).*
2 *You should* **consider** *other people's feelings.*
6 *I'm* **considering** *investing my money in oil shares.*
7 *Everyone* **considers** *him (to be) very intelligent.*
12 *I* **consider** *(think) that your action is unwise.*
13 *We must* **consider** *(think) what we ought to do.*
14 *They sat down and* **considered** *(thought about) what to do.*
23 *I* **consider** *his attitude very foolish.*
24 *If he said that, I* **consider** *him a fool.*

Consider means 'give careful thought to, think about' (**1**), (**6**), (**13**), (**14**), and in these cases is more formal and emphasises the seriousness of the speaker or situation; 'take into account' (**2**); 'regard as, **think of**' (in terms of opinion) (**7**), (**23**), (**24**); 'think, believe' (**12**), when it is again very formal.
Noun: **consideration**, careful thought, attention to others' feelings, fact to be considered – 'That's an important **consideration**'. Note 'We must take all these things into **consideration**' = 'think carefully about them all'.

realise (realised, realised)
2 *He had won, but at first he didn't* **realise** *it.*
12 *I* **realised** *that the two men were following me.*
13 *I didn't* **realise** *what time it was.*

Realise is to 'understand or become aware of' something which is not at first apparent. In all the examples given, 'notice' would be correct for an immediate reaction, but not when time has passed.
Noun: **realisation**.
Problem: He has **done** (carried out) the work. (**NOT** 'realised'. 'Realise' only remains with this meaning in a few expressions – 'He has **realised** (achieved) all his ambitions'.)

think about (thought about, thought about)
2 **Think about** *my proposal, and give me an answer.*
6 *When I* **thought about** *those people suffering so much, I decided I must do something to help them.*
13 *You must* **think about** *what you are doing.*
14 *We must* **think about** *what to do.*

Think about means 'use your mind, **consider**' (**2**) and refers to the subject of our thoughts (**2**), (**9**), (**13**), (**14**). It can also mean 'have an opinion' (**6**), but in this case it would suggest the subject had been raised previously. See **think of**.
Noun: **thought**.

think of (thought of, thought of)
2 *What do you* **think of** *this picture? Isn't it good?*
   I can't **think of** *the man's name at the moment.*
6 *I'm* **thinking of** *going to Italy for my holiday.*
9 *I don't like to* **think of** *them coming home in the dark. It worries me.*
13 **Think of** *what your parents would say.*
14 *I can't* **think of** *what to do next.*

Think of means 'have an opinion' (**2**), 'plan to' (**6**), and can also mean 'remember' (**2**), (**14**). In **9** and **13** it means '**consider** and imagine'. Where the meaning is similar to that of **think about, think about** suggests a longer thought process, similar to **consider**.
Noun: **thought**.
Problems:
I'm **thinking of** going to Italy. (**NOT** I'm thinking to go)
What do you **think of** this? (**NOT** think in/on)

understand (understood, understood)
1 *I realised that they didn't* **understand**.
2 *I don't* **understand** *this word.*
   I don't think they **understand** *their children.*
7 *I* **understood** *you to say (I thought you said) that you didn't want to come.*
12 *I* **understand** *that you can't make up your mind about it immediately.*
13 *He doesn't* **understand** *how we did it.*
14 *He doesn't* **understand** *what to do.*

Understand means 'to know or recognise the meaning of something' (**1**), (**2**), (**12**), (**13**), (**14**) but also to know the nature of a person (**2**). In **7** the use is formal, and **think**, with a different construction, is more commonly used. The verb 'comprehend' exists in English, but is rare except in the sense of **2**, 'fully understand' or 'fully sympathise with'; note, however, 'Reading Comprehension'.
Noun: **understanding**.
Problem: I don't **understand** this word. (**NOT** comprehend)

Complete the sentences, using the correct verb in the appropriate form. Consider the meaning and the structure. Do not use the same verb twice in the same sentence.

1 I know he is _____ a very promising young man, but he should _____ that his first responsibility here is to get to know the staff and _____ their point of view.
2 'What do you _____ him?'
   'Well, the trouble is he _____ nothing but work, although he doesn't _____ it, and so he doesn't _____ other people's feelings. I've tried to tell him about it, but he didn't _____.'
3 'I'm _____ going away for the weekend. Would you like to come with me?'
   'I'll have to _____ it. First, I've just _____ that we've got an exam next Monday, so I ought to revise, and there's the expense to _____. I hope you _____ how I feel.'
4 'I _____ you to say that you would be here at 11.30.'
   'Yes, but when I got to the station, I was _____ so many things that I got on the wrong train, and I had gone through two stations before I _____ where I was going.'
5 'When I started at the university, I couldn't _____ why some lecturers seemed to _____ it natural to talk without asking us what we _____ what they were saying.'
   'Perhaps they didn't _____ that you wanted to express your opinions.'

34 confuse, disgust, embarrass, shock, upset

	2	3	11	associations
	O	PO	R	
confuse	×	×		explanation, directions (mental)
disgust		×		sight, smell, bad behaviour
embarrass		×		discomfort, feeling foolish
shock		×		surprise, horror, anger
upset	×	×	×	crying, worry, sickness

Note that all the verbs in this group are commonly found in the passive construction – I was **confused**, I was **disgusted**, etc., and adjectives are formed – **confusing**, **disgusting**, **embarrassing**, etc., describing the reason for the reaction.

confuse (confused, confused)

2 *Don't* **confuse** *the issue by mentioning irrelevant details.*
3 *His explanation* **confused** *the students because it contradicted what a previous teacher had told them.*

Confuse means 'to make less clear', 'make it more difficult for other people to understand'; sometimes on purpose.
A person who is **confused** generally has an uncertain expression, or 'frowns', producing lines in the forehead.
Noun: **confusion**, disorder, state of being **confused**.

disgust

3 *The way they treated the poor old man* **disgusted** *me.*
The dirt in the room and the scraps of food left in the kitchen **disgusted** *me.*

Disgust means 'to produce a strong reaction against behaviour or what we see, smell', etc.
A person who is **disgusted** may be angry, or show signs of nausea with the mouth or nose.
Noun: **disgust**.

embarrass

3 *He* **embarrassed** *her by talking about their private life in front of their friends.*

Embarrass is 'to make people uncomfortable by what you do or say'.
People who are **embarrassed** usually 'blush' (their faces go pink or red) and look down.
Noun: **embarrassment**.
Problems:
She's going **to have a baby**/She is **pregnant**. (**NOT** She's embarrassed)
I was **embarrassed** when she mentioned my dirty clothes (**NOT** confused)

shock

3 *His sudden death* **shocked** *me.*

Shock means 'to produce a strong emotional reaction because of bad news, etc.', and often because the event occurs suddenly.
A person who is **shocked** expresses horror, great surprise, etc. A person very seriously affected by events (e.g. the mental effect of an accident) is 'suffering from **shock**'.
Noun: **shock**, the cause of the emotional reaction, also the force of an explosion, charge of electricity – 'electric **shock**'. But note problems.
Problems:
The car **crashed**. (**NOT** shocked)
The electric cable gave him a shock. (**NOT** shocked him)

upset (upset, upset)

2 *The cat jumped on the table and* **upset** *the wine.*
3 *You shouldn't have spoken to him so unkindly. You've* **upset** *him.*
11 *Don't* **upset** *yourself about it. It wasn't your fault.*

Upset can mean 'turn over, causing confusion' (The change **upset** my plans) or as in **2**, with a personal object it means 'worry, cause an emotional reaction'.
A person who is **upset** may cry or feel ill, though the reaction is not usually as strong as that of someone who is **disgusted** or **shocked**.
Noun: **upset**, usually not a very important state of confusion or physical illness (e.g. stomach **upset**).
Note that the stress falls on the first syllable in the noun and the second syllable in the verb.
Problem: She was **upset** when her cat died. (**NOT** disgusted)

The following indicate situations where the person's reaction could be described by 'I was **confused**', 'She was **disgusted**', etc. Make a phrase of this kind for each situation which best describes the person's reaction.

1 She pointed out that I was wearing one black shoe and one brown one.
2 The police rang to say his uncle had been killed in a car crash.
3 When I went into the kitchen I saw that a rat had been there.
4 I didn't know what to think, because the two of them were giving me quite different explanations of what had happened.
5 She found her little bird dead in its cage this morning.

35 cure, heal, mend, repair, solve

	1	2	3	4	associations
	−O	O	PO	2O	
cure (of 4)		×	×	×	a cold, disease
heal (of 4)	×	×	(×)	(×)	a wound, a cut
mend		×			clothes, shoes, a fence
repair		×			shoes, a car, any machine, a road
solve		×			a puzzle, crossword, a problem

cure (cured, cured)
2 *This medicine will* **cure** *your cough.*
3 *This should* **cure** *you.*
4 *The new drug* **cured** *him* **of** *his disease.*

Cure is normally associated with **solving** health problems, though it can also be used in phrases like 'cure (= **solve** the problem of) unemployment'.
Noun: **cure**, return to health, drug or medicine that **cures** or solution that **solves** certain problems.
Problem: He is being **treated** by a doctor. (**NOT** 'cured', because he would no longer need treatment.)

heal
1 *The wound will* **heal** *in time.*
2 *Her patience helped to* **heal** *the disagreement between them.*

Heal is most commonly used in **1** to mean 'become healthy again', especially for wounds and cuts. In **2** it can be used to mean '**solve** problems of personal relationships'. It is an alternative to **cure** (3), (4), but not often used in modern English.
Noun: **health**, the state of being well – 'in good **health**' (uncountable).
Problem: That cut will **heal** naturally. (**NOT** cure)

mend
2 *I'll* **mend** *your socks. There are one or two with holes in them.*

Mend and **repair** are very similar, but **mend** suggests 'by hand', without the use of machinery, and is more appropriate, for example, for sewing, using a hammer.

repair
2 *How much did the garage charge you to* **repair** *(do the* **repairs** *to) your car?*

Repair implies technical skill, the use of machinery and possibly a number of workers. One person could **mend** a fence or perhaps a road, filling in a hole; a number would be needed to **repair** a road, providing a new surface.
Noun: **repairs** (plural).
Problem: We've come to **repair** (do the **repairs** to) your house. (**NOT** mend)

solve (solved, solved)
2 *That doesn't **solve** the problem.*

Solve means 'find the answer to' a problem where there is an answer. It requires mental, or a combination of mental and physical, ability.
Noun: **solution**, answer to problem, puzzle, etc.

Complete the sentences, using the correct verb in the appropriate form. Consider the meaning and the structure.

1 I'm glad to see that your wound has _____.
2 So far doctors have not discovered any drug that will _____ the common cold.
3 Can you _____ my shirt? I've torn it.
4 How much would you charge to _____ my washing machine?
5 It was not an easy problem to _____.

36 do, make

	1	2	4	7	16	17	23	24
	−O	O	2O	OI	NC	VC	OAC	ONC
do	×	×	×			×		
make		×	×	×	×		×	×

do (did, done)
1   *That won't **do**. It's not big enough.*
2   *I want you to **do** these exercises for homework.*
4   *That won't **do** you any harm.*
17 *I thought he **did** well in the race.*

make (made, made)
2   *Look! I've **made** a cake.*
4   *I'd like to **make** you an offer.*
7   *He **made** us write it out a hundred times.*
    *They were **made** to write it out a hundred times.*
16 *Two and two **make** four.*
23 *You'll **make** her angry.*
24 *He'll **make** her a good husband.*

Noun: **make**, object, especially car, **made** by a certain firm – 'What **make** is your car? – A Ford.'.
Problems:
I **took** some photographs. (**NOT** made)
I **packed** my cases before going on holiday. (**NOT** made)
This factory **makes** furniture. (**NOT** 'fabricates' – fabricate means '**make** something artificial or false' or '**make** artificially'.)
It **is** six years since I saw him. (**NOT** It makes six years . . .)

As a general rule, **do** tends to relate to actions, **make** to causing, creating or constructing, though in the examples given **do** may mean 'be enough, be suitable' (**1**), **make** may mean 'be equal to . . .' (**16**) or 'prove . . . to her' (**24**). In practice, it is necessary to learn the list of common expressions that follows, because the correct verb must usually be remembered from the context rather than from a definition.

Note the change in the form of the infinitive after **make** in active and passive (**7**); in the passive it takes 'to'.

do

better	good	repairs
one's best	harm	right
business	homework	a service
damage	an injury	wonders
one's duty	a job	work
evil	justice (to)	worse
an exercise	a kindness	one's worst
a favour	an operation	wrong

make

an appointment	faces (at)	a report (on) (to)
arrangements	a fool (of)	a request
attacks (on)	friends (with)	room (for)
the best (of)	fun (of)	a search (for)
certain (of, about)	a fuss (about)	a speech
a change	a guess	a success (of)
a choice	haste	sure (of)
a complaint	a journey	a trip
a confession	a mistake	trouble (for)
a decision	money	use (of)
a demand	the most (of)	a voyage
a difference (to)	a movement	war (on)
a discovery	an offer	way (for)
an effort	peace (with)	(someone) welcome
enquiries	preparations	work (for others)
an escape	a profit	
an excuse (for)	progress	

Complete the sentences, using the appropriate verb in the correct form. Try to decide on the right verb from memory, and only refer to the list given if it is absolutely necessary.

A: I see the Civil Service are _____ preparations to go on strike next week. The Government has _____ them an offer of 7%, but they say it's not enough. If they are public servants they should _____ their duty and not _____ trouble for everyone else.

B: I don't think you _____ justice to them. After all, they don't _____ much money, compared with people in industry. Everyone _____ fun of them and the newspapers have _____ a lot of attacks on them recently, but most of them _____ their jobs well. They have to be very patient when the public _____ complaints about them.

A: If the Government closed half the offices, they would be _____ us all a favour. If those bureaucrats had to _____ a profit every year in order to _____ a success of their jobs, it would _____ a difference to them. They'd _____ their best, instead of _____ work for other people because they're too lazy to _____ their own work properly.

B: I'm not _____ excuses for them, but you can't expect them to _____ more than they're paid to do. They don't _____ the decisions they have to carry out.

37 drop, fall, sink, spill

	1	2	15	17
	−O	O	AC	VC
drop	×	×		
fall	×		×	×
sink	×	×		×
spill	×	×		

drop (dropped, dropped)
1 *The wind has* **dropped**.
2 *You've* **dropped** *your glove*.

Drop is normally used as in **2** to mean 'let **fall** accidentally', but we prefer **spill** for liquids. It is associated with a number of phrases: '**drop** the subject' = not talk about it any more; '**drop** someone from a team' = replace him/her with another person; '**drop** someone off' = given them a lift and leave them at an agreed place. In usage (**1**), **fall** is more common except for 'the wind', 'your voice', 'fruit falling from a tree'.
Problem: I've **dropped** my handkerchief. (**NOT** 'let it fall', unless you did it deliberately to attract attention, hoping someone would pick it up!)

fall (fell, fallen)
1 *Prices are* **falling**.
15 *He* **fell** *asleep*.
17 *They* **fell** *in love*.

Fall means 'go down freely', but compare 'He **fell** (down) (by accident) and hurt himself' and 'He went down the stairs (without **falling**)'. Note the phrases in **15** and **17** and also 'The Government has **fallen**' (can no longer govern); 'The city has **fallen**' (has been captured). See **drop**.
Noun: **fall**, the act of **falling**, decrease in prices, temperature, etc., autumn (in USA).

sink (sank, sunk)
1 *The ship is* **sinking**.
2 *The torpedo* **sank** *the ship*.
17 *She* **sank** *to the ground, exhausted*.

Sink is normally associated with 'going down' (**1**) and 'sending down (**2**) in liquid'. It can also mean 'go down gradually' (**17**); in this case, 'she **fell** to the ground', would be a more sudden movement.

Problems:
The stone **sank** to the bottom of the pool. (**NOT** fell)
The ship **sank**. (**NOT** drowned)

spill (spilt/spilled, spilt/spilled)
1 *The coffee **spilt** on to the carpet.*
2 *Don't **spill** the beer!*

Spill relates to **sink** as **drop** relates to **fall**; it normally refers only to liquids and means 'drop liquid'; but can be used (**1**) to suggest liquid **falling**. Compare **sink** (**1**), where a solid object goes down in liquid.
Problem:
I've **spilt** some coffee on my dress. (**NOT** dropped)
But note: I've **dropped** the coffee cups on the floor. (**NOT** spilt)

Complete the sentences, using the correct verb in the appropriate form. Consider the meaning and the structure.

1 She had _____ asleep but she woke up when he _____ the frying pan on the floor.
2 A lot of blood is being _____ in this war. The enemy _____ two of our ships last week.
3 Heavy rain was _____.
4 He _____ the stone into the water and it _____ to the bottom of the pool.
5 He _____ into an armchair, very tired. 'Let's _____ the subject,' he said.
6 The water from the basin _____ over the edge on to the floor.

38 explain, notice, remark, report

	1	2	4	6	7/9	11	12	13
	−O	O	2O	G	OI/P	R	TH	QW
explain (to 4)	×	×	×			×	×	×
notice	×	×			×		×	×
remark	×						×	
report (on 2, to 4)	×	×	×	×			×	×

explain
1 *I don't understand the rules, but I'm sure the experts will **explain** (them to you).*
2 *I can't **explain** it. It's never happened before.*
4 *The boss will **explain** it to you.*
11 *He was trying to tell us what happened but he couldn't **explain** himself clearly.*
12 *They **explained** that they could not ring us because they had lost their own telephone number.*
13 *Can you **explain** how it happened?*

Explain is to 'make clear (to someone)', 'show how something works', either in speech or writing.
Noun: **explanation**.
Problem: They **explained** the situation to us. (**NOT** explained us the situation)

notice (noticed, noticed)
1   *I was wearing a new dress, but he didn't even* **notice**.
2   *Did you* **notice** *anything strange on the night of the robbery?*
7/9 *I didn't* **notice** *them go/going out.*
12   *She* **noticed** *that the ornament on the table was missing.*
13   *I didn't* **notice** *what time it was.*

Notice is 'to pay attention (to someone/something) and see'.
Noun: **notice**, information given to the public – 'a **notice** on the wall', '**notice** board', (but 'the news', **NOT** 'notices', in the newspaper), attention – 'take **notice** of' (= pay attention to), statement indicating you intend to leave – 'give **notice**' to a boss, a landlord.
Problem: I **noticed** that they were behaving strangely. (**NOT** 'remarked', unless you told someone else.)

remark
1   *'What a pretty dress!' he* **remarked**.
12   *He* **remarked** *that there seemed to be fewer people in the city this summer.*

Remark is 'to say' but not usually in answer to another person.
Noun: **remark**, something you say, an observation.

report
1   *We haven't any information yet. We're waiting for our agents to* **report**.
2   *The newspaper* **reported** *his speech.*
     I want you to **report on** *the situation in Scotland.*
4   *Have you* **reported** *the loss to the police?*
6   *They* **reported** *seeing a flying saucer.*
12   *The police have* **reported** *that the fire is spreading.*
13   *He didn't* **report** *what he saw there.*

Report is to 'give information' (to people) (on subjects), usually in an official capacity, either as a journalist or to a superior in an office.
Nouns: **report**, written or spoken for a newspaper, firm etc.; **reporter**, journalist sent to **report** on particular events.
Problem: Have you **reported** the loss to the police? (**NOT** reported the police the loss)

Complete the sentences, using the correct verb in the appropriate form. Consider the meaning and the context as well as the structure.

1 'That's a strange building,' she _____ suddenly. 'I've walked down this street a hundred times, but I've never _____ it before.'
2 One of our men _____ seeing two men outside the garage just before the car was stolen, but the owner _____ that he and his family were so interested in the programme on the TV that none of them _____ anything until after it had finished. Then they discovered that the car was missing and _____ the loss to us.

135

3 'Did you _____ anything strange happening?'
   'Well, no – that is, let me _____ myself. I had a strange feeling that something
   was wrong – I can't _____ why – and I _____ that it was odd that the light
   had gone out, but no one took any notice of what I said.'
4 When the boss _____ the new system, I _____ that everyone was quiet. Then
   Mr Andrews _____ that it seemed sensible to him, and we all agreed.
5 We had just opened the bottle of wine to celebrate Harry's birthday when the boss
   put his head round the door. I put the bottle under the table quickly and luckily he
   didn't _____. 'That was an awkward moment,' Harry _____.
6 The newspapers have _____ that changes are expected in the Government's
   policy on capital punishment. 'No change could take place without a debate in
   parliament,' the Minister _____.

39 fail, lose, miss

	1	2	4	5	6	associations
	−O	O	2O	I	G	
fail	×	×		×		harvest, exam
lose	×	×	×			money, time, interest, game
miss	×	×			×	train, programme, target

fail
1 *The harvest has* **failed** *this year.*
2 *I'm sorry you* **failed** *the exam.*
5 *They* **failed** *to warn me in time.*

Fail means 'not succeed, not produce the expected result' (**1**), (**5**), and 'not pass', 'not
succeed in' (**2**). It can be used with a personal object but 'he **failed** me' is more serious
and formal and less common than 'he let me down', expressing lack of help, support.
Noun: **failure**, lack of success, person or thing that **fails**, state of not producing
normal result – 'heart **failure**', when the heart stops.
Problems:
I **failed** the exam. (**NOT** 'lost' or 'missed')
I **made a mistake** in question 3. (**NOT** I failed the question)

lose (lost, lost)
1 *I did my best, but I* **lost** *(the game).*
2 *The plane gradually* **lost** *height as it came in to land.*
   I've **lost** *my watch.*
4 *This mistake* **lost** *us the game.*

Lose is generally the opposite of 'win' (**1**), (**4**) or 'find' (**2**), but can also mean 'have less
of' (**2**). Note the associations given above, and also '**lose** your way', get **lost**; '**lose**
your temper', become very angry.
Noun: **loss**, opposite of 'profit', fact of **losing** something (financial, personal,
emotional).

136

miss
1 *He fired at the target, but* **missed**.
2 *I* **missed** *the train, because I arrived late at the station.*
  I **missed** *you while you were away.*
6 *I wouldn't like to* **miss** *(seeing) that programme.*

Miss usually means '**fail** to hit, catch or see', but it can also mean 'feel the lack or absence of a person or thing' (**2**). In general, it is best separated from **lose** by context and association, but does not usually act as the opposite of 'find' or 'win'.
Noun: **miss**, inaccurate shot, **failure** to catch, etc.
Problems:
I shot at the target, but **missed**. (**NOT** failed)
Hurry, or you'll **miss** the train. (**NOT** lose)

Complete the sentences, using the correct verb in the appropriate form. Consider the meaning and the context, as well as the structure.

1 The crops have _____ this year, and the farmers have _____ a lot of money.
2 I _____ the exam because I _____ so many classes toward the end of term.
3 Robson is going to take the penalty. If he _____, United may _____ the match.
4 McEnroe has _____ two easy shots. He doesn't look happy, and of course he hates _____, but on this occasion . . .
5 I'd hate to _____ that programme. Hurry up, or we'll _____ the train, and not get home in time to see it.
6 I _____ him while he was away, but I couldn't write to him because I'd _____ his address.
7 I don't see why you _____ the exam.
8 I _____ the first half of the play because I arrived late at the theatre and by that time I had _____ interest.

40 gaze, glance, look at, regard, stare, watch

	1	2	7	9	13	14	17	25	26
	−O	O	OI	OP	QW	QWI	VC	OVC	OAS
gaze		×					×		
glance (at 2)		×					×		
look at		×		×				×	
regard								×	×
stare (at 2)	×	×							
watch	×	×	×	×	×	×			

gaze (gazed, gazed)
2   *They were* **gazing at** *the beautiful view.*
17 *They* **gazed** *into each other's eyes.*

Gaze (at) is to 'look at in contemplation, with wonder, affection, admiration, etc.'
Compare 'stare'.
Noun: **gaze**, look.

glance (glanced, glanced)
2   *He* **glanced at** *me as he went by and then walked on down the street.*
17 *We* **glanced** *round the room, but didn't see her, and so we came away.*

Glance (at) is to 'look at for a moment'. Note that 'glimpse' means to 'see for a moment' ('I glimpsed them as they went past the window, but they were soon out of sight').
Noun: **glance**, look.
Problem: He **glanced** at his watch. (**NOT** glimpsed)

look at
2   **Look at** *me!*
9   **Look at** *them running through the garden.*
25 *I must say I* **look at** *the problem differently.*

Note that the equivalent for **1** is **Look! Regard** could be used in place of **look at** (**25**), but is more formal. Both suggest 'consider, think of'. **Look at** requires a conscious effort; 'see' does not.
Noun: **look**.
Problems:
Look! (**NOT** Look at!)
Look at me! (**NOT** See me!)

regard
25 *She* **regarded** *me thoughtfully.*
26 *I* **regard** *it as a serious matter.*

Regard means 'look at' in the most common sense in **25**, though it is more literary, and suggests a longer **look**. Note that this verb requires an adverb – here, 'thoughtfully'. In **26** it means 'consider' but compare: 'I consider it to be a serious matter'.
Noun: **regard**, long look (now uncommon) and respect, respectful consideration, but this is only found commonly now in the expression 'My **regards** (best wishes) to your family'.

stare (stared, stared)
1   *Don't* **stare!** *It's rude.*
2   *He* **stared at** *me in horror.*

Stare (at) often suggests rudeness, aggression, a long unwelcome look, but this may be caused by surprise, horror, etc.
Noun: **stare**.
Problem: That man keeps **staring** at me, and I don't like it. (**NOT** 'gazing', which would be inoffensive.)

watch
1 *I never play well when my parents are* **watching**.
2 **Watch** *me! I'm going to jump over the wall.*
7 **Watch** *them (as they) come round the corner!*
9 *We* **watched** *them playing tennis for half an hour.*
13 **Watch** *how I put the machine together.*
14 **Watch** *how to do it, so you can do it yourself.*

Watch means 'look at with attention' and can also mean 'look at carefully' – '**Watch** the baby while I'm away' and 'take care of' – 'You should **watch** your health'. Note the phrase '**Watch** your step' = 'Be careful', either when walking or in general behaviour.
Nouns: **watch**, fixed attention – 'be on the **watch** for', as well as small clock normally worn on the wrist; **watchman**, guard on a building, usually at night.
Problem: It was so horrible that I couldn't **watch** it. (**NOT** see it)

Complete the sentences, using the correct verb in the appropriate form. Consider the meaning and the context, as well as the structure. Do not use **look at** if a more precise word exists.

1 I can't stand people _____ at me in restaurants. I _____ it as very impolite.
2 'How can you sit there _____ TV on a night like this?', she said, and went out into the garden to _____ at the stars.
3 If you want to learn how to do it, _____ carefully how I do it!
4 _____ at those children running over my flower-beds!
5 He _____ at the people _____ him through the window for a moment, and then went on working.
6 We _____ the workmen repairing the road for a few minutes this morning. At least, one of them was working. Another was _____ into the distance with a sweet expression on his face. A third one _____ at us for a moment, and turned away. But the fourth obviously _____ our presence there as a nuisance, because he said, 'What are you _____ at us for? Haven't you got any work to do?'

41 give up, leave, resign, retire

	1	2	6	11
	−O	O	G	R
give up	×	×	×	
leave	×	×		
resign (from 2)	×	×		×
retire (from 2)	×	×		

give up (gave up, given up)
1 *He* **gave up** *half way through the race.*
2 *He* **gave up** *his job and went abroad.*
6 *She's* **given up** *smoking.*

Give up means 'to stop doing something or working at something' (**6**), 'to stop trying, making an effort' (**1**), 'to abandon, have no longer' (**2**).
Problem: I've **given up** smoking. (**NOT** left)

leave (**left, left**)
1 *Why are you* **leaving** *so early?*
2 *He has* **left** *his wife.*
   Leave *a message for me at the office.*
   Leave *it till tomorrow. It's not important.*

Leave means 'go away (from)' but also 'cause to remain behind' or 'not do, touch' (**2**).
Noun: **leave**, permission to be absent, especially in government or army service – 'go on **leave**, be on **leave**', and time spent on holiday, etc.
Problems:
I have **left** my books at home. (**NOT** forgotten)
They **left** for Paris this morning. (**NOT** parted)
Don't **let** them come in! (**NOT** leave)
Don't **let/leave go of** it! Hold on to it! (**NOT** Don't leave it!)

resign
1 *I had a row with the boss, and so I* **resigned**.
2 *He* **resigned** *his post in the Government because he didn't agree with their policy.*
   He **resigned from** *the party because he didn't agree with their policy.*
11 *There was no sign of her anywhere, so he* **resigned** *himself to waiting.*

See **retire**. If you **resign** yourself to something, you accept it because you have no choice; if this state of mind becomes permanent, you '**are resigned**'.
Noun: **resignation**, the act of giving up a job, leaving a group, or state of mind accepting things without hope.

retire (**retired, retired**)
1 *I'm* **retiring** *next year, when I am 65.*
2 *I'm* **retiring from** *my job next year.*

You **retire** when you reach a certain age, but you **resign** because you want to **leave** the job.
Noun: **retirement**, the state of being **retired**, or of **retiring**.
Problem: Please **take** the plates **away**. (**NOT** retire the plates)

Complete the sentences, using the correct verb in the appropriate form. Consider the meaning as well as the structure.

1 Don't _____ hope! You can still get there on time.
2 I _____ from the company because I was not happy there.
3 I'm _____ now but I'll be back this evening.
4 He's _____ playing football because he's too old.
5 When her husband _____ home, she did not realise that he was _____ her and the children for ever; now she has _____ herself to never seeing him again.
6 He's only 39 but he's already worrying about the pension he will get when he _____ from the firm.
7 Don't _____. You can still win!
8 What are you going to do when you retire?

I'm going to keep active. I'm not going to _____ myself to collecting my pension and growing old.

42 relax, remain, rest, stay

	1	2	15	16	17	25
	−O	O	AC	NC	VC	OVC
relax	×	×				
remain	×		×	×	×	
rest	×	×				×
stay	×		×		×	

relax

1 *Take things easy!* **Relax***!*
2 **Relax** *your muscles and imagine you are resting in a comfortable bed.*

Relax means to 'stop worrying', 'become or make less tense'. Compare **rest**. We **rest** because we are tired, but **relax** because we are worried, in a nervous state.
Noun: **relaxation**, this state of being **relaxed** or a means of providing this state. Note: 'I've come on holiday for **relaxation**' (**NOT** 'for a relax').

remain

1 *When the party was over, the other guests went home and only John* **remained***.*
15 *Even after the meal, he* **remained** *hungry (he was still hungry).*
16 *He* **remained** *a countryman at heart, although he had moved to the city.*
17 *He* **remained** (**stayed**) *in the same job all his life.*

Remain is more formal than **stay**, and is more commonly found in literary contexts (**16**) than in **15** or **17**. It differs from **stay** in **1** because of the contrast with 'the other guests', the idea of 'being left behind'.
Nouns: **remainder**, what is left behind; **remains**, parts of something left, destroyed or dead.
Problem: This is all the money that **remains**. (**NOT** rests)

rest

1 *I'm tired. I'm going to lie down and* **rest***.*
2 **Rest** *your tired feet. Sit down!*
25 **Rest** *your head on my shoulder.*

Rest means 'not do anything' because of tiredness, illness, etc. (**1**) or 'allow to **rest**' (**2**), but can also mean 'lean against', 'support yourself on' (**25**).
Noun: **rest**, period of time spent **resting**; support, for example for camera. Note 'the **rest**', what **remains**, the others, similar to 'the **remainder**' but more common, without the idea of being left behind.

stay

1   *She's staying at the hotel in the village.*
15 Stay *still, and stop jumping about!*
17 *He stayed in the same job all his life.*

Stay means 'live in a place for a time' (**1**) or 'continue to be' (**2**). In **17** it means **remain**, and could be substituted for **remain** in **16**, but would be less formal.
Noun: **stay**, usually period of time spent (living) in a hospital, hotel, etc. – 'Enjoy your **stay**'.
Problems:
She's **staying** at her cousin's house for a week. (**NOT** 'remaining', unless there is a contrast with others who have left.)

Complete the sentences, using the correct verb in the appropriate form. Consider the meaning and the structure.

1 I'm the only member of the family that _____, now that my brothers have died.
2 You've been working too hard, and you need to _____. Why don't you go on holiday or _____ on the golf course for a while.
3 A lot of foreigners were _____ at the hotel last week, but now his friends have gone away and he's the only one that _____.
4 He _____ still, his head in his hands, for a long time.
5 Now _____ your whole body in preparation for the next exercise. Don't lie down! You'll have time to _____ afterwards.
6 'It's amazing that you've _____ a teacher all your life. Have you no ambition?' 'Yes, but I like my work.'

Key to structural abbreviations

	Abbreviation	Structure	Example
1	−O	No object	*They are working*
2	O	Object	*He drives* a car.
3	PO	Personal object	*She loves* him.
4	2O	Two objects	*He gave* me the book.
5	I	Infinitive	*They helped* to build *the house.*
6	G	Gerund	*He likes* singing.
7	OI	Object – infinitive	*Tell* him to come *here.*
8	OG	Object – gerund	*I don't like* them (their) behaving *badly.*
9	OP	Object – present participle	*I watched* them going *away.*
10	2OI	Two objects – infinitive	*I found* them a ball to play *with.*
11	R	Reflexive	*She has hurt* herself.
12	TH	**that** clause	*He admitted* that he was guilty.
13	QW	Question word	*I know* where *he is.*
14	QWI	Question word – infinitive	*I know* what to do.
15	AC	Adjective complement	*It's getting* dark.
16	NC	Noun complement	*He proved* a good worker.
17	VC	Adverbial complement	*He drove* to the station.
18	AS	**as**	*He works* as *a salesman.*
19	SO	**so**	*I hope* so.
20	OTH	Object – **that** clause	*I told* him that he was mistaken.
21	OQW	Object – question word	*Ask* her where *she lives.*
22	OQWI	Object – question word – infinitive	*Ask* them what to do.
23	OAC	Object – adjective complement	*I considered* him foolish.
24	ONC	Object – noun complement	*They elected* him president.
25	OVC	Object – adverbial complement	*He's worn* a hole in his sock.
26	OAS	Object – **as**	*They chose* him as *their leader.*
27	OSO	Object – **so**	*I told* you so.
28	RO	Reflexive – object	*You'll do* yourself an injury.
29	RI	Reflexive – infinitive	*Let* yourself go!
30	RAC	Reflexive – adjective complement	*I find* myself unable to answer.
31	RNC	Reflexive – noun complement	*He proved* himself a good worker.
32	RVC	Reflexive – adverbial complement	*He found* himself in hospital.

Index to Part B — Verbs

Note that numbers refer to verb group headings